# FAITH ON TRIAL IN RUSSIA

# FAITH ON TRIAL
# IN RUSSIA

by

## MICHAEL BOURDEAUX

Research Fellow,
Centre for International Studies
London School of Economics and Political Science

HODDER AND STOUGHTON
LONDON   SYDNEY   AUCKLAND   TORONTO

To Mark and his Godparents

"I stand before you with a calm and clear conscience; I have honourably obeyed all the civil laws and faithfully respected the laws of God ... I do not see you, Comrade Judges, Comrade Prosecutor and all here present, as my enemies; you're my brothers and sisters in the human race ... Today here, as in Pilate's day, Christ our Saviour is being judged."

Georgi Vins at his trial in 1966

# CONTENTS

# Chapter I

## A DEMONSTRATION IN MAY

May 16, 1966, was a glorious day of spring sunshine in Moscow, and the usual city crowds, swollen by tourists from every part of the Soviet Union and many other countries, strolled through the streets. But in Old Square, dominated on one side by the drab walls of the offices of the Central Committee of the Communist Party, there were noticeably more people than usual, many of them obviously not Muscovites.

In fact, something totally abnormal in modern Russia was about to take place—something that had not happened in Moscow for fifty years—something that the astounded onlookers would hardly be able to believe they were witnessing. For in that crowd were five hundred people who had been sent to Moscow by Baptist congregations all over the Soviet Union—from one hundred and thirty towns and cities.

Slowly they converged on the Central Committee building, assembling in an orderly manner, but inevitably obstructing the pavement. Passers-by, sensing that something unusual was about to happen, stopped to watch. As the purpose of the five hundred became more obvious, the onlookers could scarcely believe their senses. In London, Paris or Washington it would have caused little stir, but in Moscow things like this simply do not happen.

For, unless their eyes were deceiving them, they were witnessing nothing other than a mass *demonstration*.

When the crowd finally formed up, the demonstrators moved into the central courtyard. A handful of their leaders separated themselves from the mass and approached the main doors of the building, one of them carrying in his hand a letter.

Who were these demonstrators and what did that letter contain?

The demonstrators were delegates who had been elected to represent Baptist congregations in one hundred and thirty areas all over the Soviet Union, from Brest on the Polish frontier, six hundred miles west of Moscow, to Vladivostok on the Pacific coast, over four thousand miles east of the capital.

The letter the leaders had with them was addressed to the Central Committee of the Communist Party. It contained a request for permission to hold a congress of representatives from all the Baptist congregations of the Soviet Union. It went on to ask for recognition of the organization which these delegates represented, the Council of Churches of the Evangelical Christians and Baptists. Then the document begged that religious persecution should cease, that state interference in internal church affairs should discontinue and that Christians imprisoned for their faith should be released. Finally, there was the request that Soviet Citizens should have the right to teach religion and be instructed in it.

The leaders of the five hundred delegates asked to see Mr. Brezhnev, Chairman of the Central Committee, who had an office in the building. But they were not allowed into the building to see anyone, although they were able to leave their petition with a receptionist at the door. The whole crowd waited and waited, patiently and in an orderly fashion, the whole day through and right on into the long, light evening. Though some of the delegates were exhausted from their long journeys, not one moved off during the short night to find shelter. Most of them had met each other for the first time that day, but they felt a tremendous solidarity and sense of common purpose. For the first time they realized the strength of their movement and discovered in talking together during those long hours just how vast an area of the Soviet Union was represented in their ranks. They knew that what they were doing might well result in their arrest and imprisonment, but they had reached a point at which they did not feel they could remain silent any longer.

Early the next morning, Tuesday, they discovered to their joy that they were being joined by some of the braver members of the Moscow Baptist Church. They had heard about what was happening and about a hundred took time off from work to come and add their support. It started to rain, but the crowd moved out of the courtyard and back into Old Square outside, to ensure that the demonstration was a truly public one. Casual passers-by, tourists, children on the way to school, men and women going to work paused to gaze at the unusual sight. Some lingered to ask what it was all about. Then detachments of soldiers, police and state security (KGB) officials were driven up. They formed a ring around the Baptist demonstrators to prevent any conversation between them and the passers-by.

At mid-day an official from the Central Committee building appeared and said that ten leaders could come in. He ordered all the rest to go home at once. The leaders accepted his invitation, but the crowd did not. The people were of one mind—and that mind told them to stay until their leaders came safely back. After all, they knew that for months the State Security had been trying to discover the whereabouts of these very leaders. Now here they were, voluntarily stepping forward into the jaws of one of the most important official buildings in Moscow.

The call went up for public prayer for those who had been taken into the grim, impersonal building. Its fervour astounded the onlookers, who had until a moment before been part of the casual gaiety of Moscow's May-time streets. Rapidly the crowd of onlookers started to swell.

Suddenly a fleet of empty buses appeared. The drivers nosed them with difficulty through the crowd, but the ring of police rapidly broke up to make way for them. Instead of re-forming their ranks, the police and soldiers, in full view of the onlookers, suddenly launched into a violent assault on the six hundred praying Baptists. Using truncheons, bottles and any other handy weapons, they started to hit them indiscriminately over the head, smash their arms, or grab the collars of their clothes with such violence that either their suits and dresses were ripped open or the victims were nearly choked from the force which was used. The police started throwing the demonstrators into the buses, which moved off as soon as they were full.

The Baptists rapidly took action themselves. They did not, of course, offer any physical retaliation. They knew that if they did, it would be used later in accusations against them. But they had a much deeper reason for restraint—their whole belief and philosophy of life were founded on a doctrine of non-violence. Those who were not victims of the first assault linked arms to form a human chain and took up the strains of one of their best-loved hymns, 'For the evangelical faith'. They sang so fervently that the words rang out over the square, clearly audible above the hubbub of screaming policemen, victims crying out in pain, the shouts of the crowd of onlookers and the roar of traffic. The singing went on even as the police violently tore apart the groups of Baptists and bundled them into the buses.

'The best days of our life, the radiant strength of our young spring we shall dedicate to Jesus . . . Many perish in sin, but we shall bring them the good news'—these words resounded through the square. But the singing became thinner and thinner as organized detachments of people in civilian clothes joined in to speed up the process of dispersing the demonstration. They used their fists freely to isolate their victims from the crowd. The last voices were choked and the singing died as the final group was hurled into a bus and driven away.

Yet even this did not quench the spirit of these people. The busloads of Baptists who had been removed from Old Square were too numerous to be accommodated at once in the cells of the police station to which they were driven. They were herded into the courtyard of the building and kept standing while arrangements were being made. Far from being deterred by their experiences, they decided to use the time in the best possible way, so they held an impromptu service of worship right there as an act of witness to the Moscow police force. They sang hymns and recited poetry aloud. One had even managed to retain a precious Bible through all the scuffles and he used it now to read from the Scriptures. Strangely, perhaps out of curiosity, the police allowed the worship to continue. But soon the arrangements were complete. Detachments of police came forward, broke up the Baptists into small groups and dispersed them to all the different prisons of Moscow.

Now, in isolation, the interrogations began . . .

The security police wanted to identify and silence once and for all the leaders of this movement. For five years these people had been pressing their case for religious freedom more and more openly. Their movement had now changed from being a minor nuisance confined mainly to the provinces to something approaching a major national scandal—a demonstration on the streets of Moscow, attracting the attention not only of thousands of Soviet citizens, but of foreign tourists as well. It was time to do something decisive. All the leading spirits must be rounded up. The interrogation would be hard.

In fact, it proved to be easier than they had expected. In the first place, they already held in custody some of the leaders they wanted, who had virtually given themselves up by their bold request for an interview with Mr. Brezhnev on May 16.

Then, on May 19, two of the men who had been on the black-list of the security forces for several years walked into the Central Committee building and presented themselves at the reception desk. One of these men, Georgi Vins, related what followed in evidence at his trial six months later:

I must recount how I was arrested. On May 19 I went, with Brother M. I. Khorev, to the reception desk of the Central Committee of the Communist Party. On the instructions of the Council of Churches, I was to find out what had happened to the delegation of believers who had assembled on Old Square in Moscow on May 16–17. We were given a pass and after about twenty minutes' conversation we were told to return for a reply in an hour-and-a-half. We went back a second time and were received by Stroganov, head of reception at the Central Committee building. He talked with us, but his words sounded strange: "You Baptists are a bad lot—the Tsarist Government was right to chase you out. The State won't let you have a congress under your leadership."

When we emerged from the building a black car drove up, several men grabbed Brother Khorev and they pinioned his arms behind his back. An amiable-looking man came up to me, addressed me by my first name and patronymic[1] and said he wanted to have a talk with me. I said I was prepared to go along, but I asked why they had pinioned Khorev's arms. He turned to the men who had arrested Khorev and told them to let his arms go. They put us into different cars and they told me they were taking me for a chat. I asked what was happening to Khorev and the answer came, "You'll find out later."

The man who had arrested me was Major-General Boiko of the State Security Committee. They took me along to one of its offices. Suddenly the Major-General who had promised to have a chat with me began to leave.

"What about our talk?" I asked.

"You'll be told all about it straight away," he replied, and left the room.

A police officer was then summoned and he drew up an official warrant for my arrest. I was designated to Butyrki Prison No. 2 and I was held in solitary confinement in a State Security investigation cell. The investigation itself was conducted by the State Security, though this was concealed by using the name of Boriskin, of the Public Prosecutor's office, who drew up the documents.

Even after the arrest of Georgi Vins, things still did not remain quiet outside the Central Committee buildings. More Baptists arrived and continued to hold smaller peaceful demonstrations. On Sunday, May 22, almost a week after the initial events, yet another group came and sat down on the pavement, demanding to see Mr. Brezhnev. By this time all Moscow knew what was happening. There were now foreign correspondents present outside the building, so the police acted with much less violence than they had done the previous week.

But the brutality was simply transferred to a more private setting away from the observant eyes of western reporters. That very same Sunday, even though they now had Vins in custody, the police swooped on his defenceless congregation—people who loved him dearly and had for five years been inspired by his leadership.

Georgi Vins had been the pastor of a Baptist congregation in Kiev, a city with a great Christian history and the capital of the Ukraine, situated five hundred miles south-west of Moscow. We shall discover later why it was that Vins's congregation had no regular place of worship. In the winter they used to meet in private houses, but it was never possible to accommodate the four hundred or more who wished to attend. In the summer the situation was better. They had taken to meeting in a wood by a railway junction outside the city. For three years they had met there regularly during the better weather. The local Communist authorities had been informed about it and had not interfered.

But all that changed on May 22, 1966. Obviously an order had been received from Moscow in connection with the events of the previous week. At the start of the service there were more than double the usual number of people present. Special cars and buses had brought hundreds of police, State Security men and civilian auxiliaries. The interlopers surrounded the Baptists, but kept their distance until almost the end of the service. Then, before the final blessing could be spoken, Major-General Degtyarev, the Security official in charge of the operation, gave a signal. All his underlings launched themselves forward. Apart from the sylvan setting, what happened was very similar to the events in Moscow of the previous Tuesday—except that this time it was worse, because there were many women and children present, who came in for precisely the same treatment as their menfolk.

The police tried to drive the worshippers away from the railway and in the direction of the wood. They did not want passengers on the trains to see what was happening. They need not have bothered—all the electric trains had been stopped until the operation was over.

Fewer people were arrested that day in Kiev—about thirty in all—and the other Baptists were returned to the central station by train. Here the platform had been cordoned off and surrounded by cars and hundreds of auxiliary police, in case further arrests were necessary.

The next day a delegation of Baptists went to the office of the Public Prosecutor to complain about what had happened. They were not allowed into the building, so they returned to the house of Brother G. S. Magel to pray. Within a quarter of an hour several cars drew up and Major-General Degtyarev jumped out. He ordered his men to arrest all the Baptists present and take them to preparatory investigation cells.

A crowd of onlookers had gathered outside. Degtyarev remained behind to deliver them a speech—a choice piece of oratory, in which he said that Christians were anti-Soviet criminals, debauchees, thieves, drunkards and murderers. He dragged in all the worst crimes known to have been committed in Kiev in recent weeks, including rape and the murder of a child, laying them at the door of those whom his men had just carried off. He ended by appealing to his listeners to protect their children from these monsters.

In all, about a hundred people were arrested over the two days. Many were released within a fortnight after paying heavy fines, but some were tortured during interrogation and the leaders were detained in custody to face criminal charges at a convenient time later.

The very next day after the arrests, May 24, no less than 116 people were contacted by local Baptist leaders to sign a hastily-compiled eye-witness report of these events. It is their testimony which we have used above. The compiler bitterly summarized his feelings in these words: "All this is not happening in some under-developed colonial country, nor under a fascist régime, but in a land which has been proclaiming to all the world for fifty years that it has built the most just, democratic and humanitarian society, where there is equality of all people, irrespective of race and creed."

\*      \*      \*

These events, it must be emphasized, were completely unprecedented in the Soviet Union. Decades of persecution and discrimination had never before evoked so dramatic a Christian response. Was this the birth of 'church power' in Russia, as 'student power' and 'black power' had risen to challenge Governments in the West? And was the Soviet Government disturbed or shaken by this sudden manifestation of Christian determination and solidarity? There are good grounds for answering both questions in the affirmative.

We are today in possession of a wealth of information about what is happening to Christians in Russia. This book can present only a fraction of the evidence and must exclude almost entirely a consideration of the continuing witness, indeed the spiritual revival, of the Russian Orthodox Church in recent years. As recently as May 1969 an English evangelical weekly printed these words: "We lack information about our brothers in Christ in the Soviet Union" (*Life of Faith*, May 17, 1969, p. 5). In fact, this statement is no longer true—though it would have been in 1959. In the last decade the religious situation has become one of the best-documented areas of contemporary Soviet life. This is not due to any notable effort on the part of interested churchmen in the West, but to the courage, in the face of severe physical persecution, of those Christians in Russia—Orthodox, Catholics and Protestants—who have committed their lives to fighting for human rights and basic religious liberties.

This book focuses on the heroism of a particular group of Protestants. It tells their story, and in particular the story of Georgi Vins, the young Baptist leader about whom we happen to know the most.[2]

Our studies of the Baptist and Orthodox Churches have convinced us that 'church power' has emerged on the Soviet scene over the last decade. After forty years of more or less continuous religious repression, there have recently been demonstrations, street processions, open-air services, public baptisms, the circulation of a multitude of petitions to the government, often signed by hundreds, even thousands, of people, appeals to the United Nations, to Christian leaders of the West and to world public opinion, the despatch of hundreds of documents out of the Soviet Union as evidence and the setting-up of a clandestine press which has produced regular religious journals and even whole books.

The standard atheist line in journalism published in the Soviet Union continues to be that religion is on the point of dying out or that it is the preserve solely of the old and the uneducated. But often the same newspaper, even the same article, will contain clear evidence that this is not true. For over fifty years the plan has been to strangle all organized religion and to extirpate even its vestiges from the hearts of the people. Yet events of the last decade show quite clearly that the defenders of religious freedom are much more outspoken, much more determined and ready to take risks than at any time since the Revolution. This certainly suggests an outbreak of 'church power' into the life of the Soviet nation.

If this outbreak were an isolated phenomenon, the Soviet Government might not be seriously worried about it (except that, according to our speculations, there are probably still at least fifty million Christians in the country, a very large body of public opinion indeed). But it is not isolated—and this is why Soviet statesmen are frightened.

We have to see the events outside the Central Committee building on May 16, 1966, in the context of many other public demonstrations, large and small; and of the clandestine distribution of a massive number of documents concerning a wide variety of aspects of life in the Soviet Union about which there is discontent.

One could name at least four other areas of major concern, all of which to some extent overlap with some of the others. It is far, far too early to predict whether or not these will all coalesce into one big opposition movement, but it would be surprising if the Soviet Government were not terrified that something like this might happen. It may be possible to explain some of the more brutal elements in its recent policies as irrational reactions caused by this fear—an attempt to terrorize wide sections of the population into a cowed inactivity, as in the days of Stalin and Beria.

The type of dissent most closely allied to that now being expressed in the Baptist Church is found among members of the Russian Orthodox Church. The leader of this reform movement is Archbishop Yermogen, formerly of Kaluga, now in enforced retirement. As the only man to build a cathedral in the Soviet Union (at Tashkent) since the Revolution, his reputation has for many years been high among Russian churchmen. For resolutely opposing the closure of churches in his diocese and for fighting the interference of atheists in church appointments under him, he was removed from office in 1965. His primacy of honour is now more explicit than it has ever been and he has aroused a spontaneous following among many of the outstanding Russian Orthodox Christians, old and young. Both he and some of his followers have referred to the brave stand of the Russian Baptists as a model to be followed. From time to time, as in the Diocese of Kirov in 1961–4, there have been demonstrations in which hundreds of Orthodox people have expressed their indignation against the closure and destruction of churches.

Since the sentences on the writers Andrei Sinyavsky and Yuli Daniel in 1966, there have been increasing demands among intellectuals (Christians, agnostics and atheists alike) for freedom of expression. It is hardly putting it too strongly to say that none of the best literature can now be published in the Soviet Union. Hundreds of manuscripts circulate clandestinely, some of which are translated and published when they reach the West. It is not surprising that the Soviet Government's continuing brutality towards some of its finest writers has provoked an increasingly political reaction, particularly since the invasion of Czechoslovakia in August 1968. In the present context, we are particularly interested that these repressed intellectuals are taking more and more interest in the fate of Christians. Yuri Galanskov and Alexander Ginzburg were among the principal defenders of Sinyavsky and Daniel and did much to publicize their case. Galanskov seems to have been scandalized by the treatment being accorded to the Russian Orthodox Church. He protested against it by including in his underground literary journal, *Phoenix 1966,* a long account of the persecution of monks from the Pochaev monastery over the previous six years. Now from their prison camp Daniel (a Jew), Ginzburg, Galanskov and three other sympathizers wrote in the spring of 1969: "Occasional 'lectures' delivered by the officers or by visiting speakers are, as a rule, offensive to the religious and national feelings of the political prisoners ... There is a prohibition against believers (imprisoned for religious activities) receiving religious literature. Even the Bible is forbidden."

There is now an anonymous group of people in the Soviet Union who have started to compile a *Chronicle of Current Events,* thirteen consecutive numbers of which have reached the West at the time of writing. In it they scrupulously document all the measures taken against Soviet citizens which infringe their basic human rights. Baptists and Orthodox

Christians have now started to feature prominently in this documentation.

Even more disturbing to the Soviet Government must be the recent activities of one of Russia's top atomic scientists, Academician Andrei Sakharov. He has started to delve seriously into politics and finds himself in disagreement with much of what his country has been doing, both internally and in foreign affairs. He has formulated a new world plan in which one of the main features is a grass-roots co-operation between the Soviet Union and the United States to ensure peace and to alleviate all the injustices in the poorer areas of the world. Immediately a reply came from a group of Estonians, who claimed that Sakharov had not gone nearly far enough and asked how the Soviet Government could ever hope to enforce morality now that they had overthrown Christian standards.

This brings us to the fourth area, nationalism. All problems concerned with the hundreds of ethnic minorities in the Soviet Union have been intensified since the invasion of Czechoslovakia. Estonians, Ukrainians, Crimean Tartars, Moldavians and the Muslim peoples of Central Asia now know for sure that they can hope for no general expansion of their freedom, no approved movement towards genuine democracy, while the present régime remains in office. Many people from these areas, as well as from dozens of other regions and also many Jews scattered throughout the cities of the Soviet Union, are acutely aware that they face official opposition if they wish to bring up their children in their own national or religious traditions, if they wish to write objectively about their own history, or if they desire to further the cause of literature in their own languages.

It may well be that this is potentially the most explosive subject with which the Soviet Government has to deal at present in its internal policies. And we need hardly emphasize how important the religious element is here. For example, one of the most devastating blows to the Ukraine was the liquidation of the Eastern-Rite (Greek) Catholic Church in 1946. This had about four million members in the western part of the Republic. The Soviet secret police instigated a terrorist campaign, imprisoning hundreds of the clergy, as a preliminary to a take-

over by the Russian Orthodox hierarchy. The political idea
behind this was that the loyalty of these people should be diver-
ted from Rome to Moscow. But in fact an underground Eastern-Rite Church continued to exist and it must have received
immense encouragement when, in the first half of 1968, its
sister-church in Czechoslovakia—which had been similarly
liquidated—was reconstituted and began a most vigorous activity. Discouragement was soon to follow, for in January 1969
its secret leader, Bishop Velichkovsky, was arrested, even
though he was a very sick man of seventy. A number of other
priests have suffered a similar fate.

*          *          *

There is, then, a human rights movement in the Soviet Union.
We are now able to see the emergence of 'church power' in its
context, though of course we have only been able to hint at the
importance of some of the other movements with which it is
associated. Nevertheless, we have seen enough to suggest that
the Soviet Government is frightened. We must bear this in
mind as a possible explanation for the excessive and often
contra-productive violence to which the authorities have subjected the Baptists.

The incident in Moscow which we described at the outset
was perhaps the most dramatic demonstration of discontent
which has been seen on the streets of the capital since the Revolution. As such, it is very surprising that it received little notice
in the western press at the time—eight lines tucked away in the
London *Times* and scarcely anything elsewhere. But as a feat of
organization by the Baptists the achievement was remarkable.
To bring together six hundred people from one hundred and
thirty cities even in the United States (a much smaller area than
the Soviet Union) takes some organizing ... and that is in a
country where communications are good, where people have
the money to travel and where demonstrations are legal. What
we have described occurred in a country where none of these
conditions applies—indeed, the state had been organizing an
all-out campaign against these Baptists for five years and the
demonstrators knew that to take part might well lead to arrest,
an inadequate trial and a sentence of up to three years. We may

never know how the leaders managed to bring their people together while they themselves were being hunted or were under the surveillance of the secret police. We can, however, claim that the bravery of the most active people in this movement has few parallels in the annals of twentieth-century Christian history.

This book tells their story. We shall learn what was the chain of events which led the Baptists to the Central Committee building on that day in May 1966, and we shall hear what some of the consequences were. Before we resume our narration of these recent dramatic events, we must go back to the early days of the Protestant Churches in Russia and trace the lives of some of the earlier martyrs and heroes, men without whom the present Baptist leaders would probably never have come to their commitment to the faith.

## NOTES

1. "Georgi Petrovich"—the polite form of address in Russian.

2. For an academic treatment of the subject the reader is referred to the present author's Oxford University thesis, published by Macmillan, London, in 1968 and entitled, *Religious Ferment in Russia: Protestant Opposition to Soviet Religious Policy*. In this he reproduced in full all the relevant documents known to him up to mid-1967. Some of these are here put into narrative form, but the author has rigorously excluded any "fictional" reconstructions of his own. Between mid-1967 and the end of 1969, over six hundred pages of new documents relating to the Baptist situation alone have reached us from the Soviet Union. Some of these will be found in a book edited by Xenia Howard-Johnston and Rosemary Harris, entitled, *Christian Appeals from Russia* (Hodder & Stoughton, London, 1969), but the bulk have remained unpublished and this book will draw heavily on them.

We know the situation of the Orthodox Church in no less detail. To find out about it, the reader is referred to the present author's *Patriarch and Prophets: Persecution of the Russian Orthodox Church Today* (Macmillan, London, and Praeger, New York, 1970).

*Chapter II*

# ORIGINS (1867–1917)

## Russian 'Sectarians'

The history of the Evangelical Christian and Baptist
Church in Russia, except for a short period of time, has been
the history of a people doomed to lifelong suffering, a history
of camps and imprisonments affecting fathers, children and
grandchildren . . .

Persecution has become hereditary—our grandfathers
were persecuted, our fathers were persecuted; now we ourselves are persecuted and oppressed, while our children are
suffering hardships and deprivations.

These words of Georgi Vins and his fellow-believers could
be used as a theme for the history of the Baptist movement in
Russia. Persecution of non-conforming religious minorities was
widespread in Russia long before it became rampant in the
post-revolutionary period. During the latter period, however,
its scope has broadened to include the Russian Orthodox
Church as well. As we look back over the last hundred years, it
is depressing to note how many of the perversions of justice and
denials of basic human rights under the Tsars were repeated
almost verbatim under Stalin and his successors. We shall not
attempt to write a formal history in these pages, but to give a
series of pictures to illustrate the continuity of suffering up to
the emergence in 1961 of a new human rights movement among
the Russian Baptists.

Probably fear that the monolithic unity of the Russian
Empire was threatened by religious minorities gave rise to the
official Tsarist attitude of intolerance. 'Autocracy, Orthodoxy,
Nationality'—these words symbolized the power-structure for
the Tsars (you can still see them engraved on the giant eques-

23

trian statue of Nicholas I in Leningrad). There was to be a nation of one people, cemented by Russian Orthodoxy, the established Church of the land, ruled over by a Tsar as the supreme religious and civil leader.

In fact, from the Middle Ages, when the rulers expelled the Mongol invaders and Moscow emerged as the centre of a new civilization, the Tsars fought with and sometimes subjugated hostile neighbours, incorporating them into the nation. Equally, when conditions were favourable, foreign workmen and traders settled in Russia. The old system was never completely monolithic.

Still, it was an internal event, the Great Schism of the seventeenth century, which truly made a mockery of the slogan. It was then that the 'Old Believers' split away from the official Church, after which they suffered exile and persecution. For their part, they often showed their contempt for the authorities by nurturing fanaticism, locking themselves in barns and setting fire to them in a series of ritual self-immolations.

From this sort of situation emerged the sects of Old Russia, some much more extremist than others—Dukhobors ('Spirit-Wrestlers'), Molokans ('Milk-Drinkers'), Khlysts ('Flagellants'), Skoptsy ('Castrated') and many more. This bizarre catalogue of names should not obscure the fact that there was much genuine goodness and zeal to be found in some areas of this dissent from Orthodoxy. Furthermore, sometimes fanaticism was a reaction to persecution rather than its cause.

Any American can see for himself, without setting foot outside his own country, that Russian sectarians, left to their own ways, are an enrichment to society—level-headed, hard-working and hospitable. If one goes, for example, to the lake front at Erie, Pennsylvania, at 7.30 a.m. on a Sunday morning one will be received as a welcome guest by a community of 'Priestless' Old Believers. Finding no peace in Russia, they emigrated to the U.S.A. before the Revolution. They have kept all their old traditions: the men do not shave, the women wear ankle-length peasant dresses; and when they sing, they use unharmonized mediaeval chants. Yet they have not opted out of the American way of life. They work hard and well and come to church in cars. Their children go to state schools and do well at university. Protestant 'fanatics' (to use the Soviet term) in the guise of Russian Pentecostals are seen to be equally responsible members of society by anyone who visits San Francisco and seeks them out.

The reign of Nicholas I in the nineteenth century saw the mounting of a more systematic campaign against the sectarians than anything Russia had previously known. The new penal code of 1842 reclassified the Old Believers and sectarians, describing them as 'less harmful', 'more harmful' and 'especially harmful' groups. It is interesting that the Dukhobors and the Molokans were both put into the last category, although the latter came into being as a very spiritual reaction to the excesses of the Dukhobors. The Molokans were forerunners of the Russian Baptists in the Caucasus Mountains.

The new measures introduced by the state were severe. For those in the 'especially harmful' category (which included also the 'Priestless' Old Believers), there was a ban on religious meetings and their churches were closed. In some places they lived in tight-knit communities, which were broken up by the exile of their members to Siberia and the removal of their children to families where they could be raised as Orthodox. All these tactics have been used again in recent times, though even more impersonal communist boarding schools have replaced the Orthodox adoptive parents.

None of these measures was successful and the number of dissenters continued to increase. Their number was soon to be swollen by the emergence in the second half of the nineteenth century of Protestant groups practising believers' baptism.

We must be quite clear about one thing. Remarks made above about 'religious fanaticism' in no way apply to the Russian Baptists. The inner quality of their Christian lives has been—and still is—singularly intense, but Soviet propaganda charging all kinds of malpractices is demonstrably untrue. Their virtues have often been the envy of those about them and from the time of the first conversions they have formed part of the Protestant mainstream, despite the isolation of many of their communities.

Protestantism was first brought on to Russian soil by German immigrants and by isolated Latvians, Estonians and

Englishmen. Its life as an indigenous movement began independently in three areas of Russia: the Caucasus, the Ukraine
and St. Petersburg (now Leningrad). As it took root in these
regions under quite different sets of influences, but in all three
at very nearly the same time, it seems that Russia must at that
moment have been precisely ready for this development.

The second half of the nineteenth century was an era of
extreme social ferment in Russia, when many of the forces were
already at work which were finally unleashed in the Revolution
of 1917. The publication of the Bible in the vernacular (from
1819 when the Gospels appeared), the growth of literacy, the
breakdown of the country in the Crimean War (1853–6) and
the emancipation of the serfs from slavery (1861) all con-
tributed strongly, but in very different ways, to the final prep-
aration of the soil for the growth of Protestantism.

The Russian Baptists celebrated their centenary in 1967,
taking the baptism of Nikita Voronin in the River Kura, near
Tiflis (Caucasus), as the beginning of the movement as such.
He was converted by Martin Kalveit, who had been brought up
as a Lutheran, but went on to become a convert to the Baptist
Church in Lithuania in 1858, where he underwent baptism by
immersion. Kalveit was one of a number of Protestants from
the Baltic States who had an influence on Russia at this time.
There had long been a Lutheran Church in Latvia and Estonia.
Now the Baptist faith also took root there, whence it spread
into Russia. Kalveit and Voronin gathered around them a small
but extremely powerful group of supporters. Two of them,
Vasili Ivanov and Vasili Pavlov, were destined to play a great
role in the future of the movement and we shall be hearing
much more about the latter at the end of this chapter.

Simultaneously something almost identical was happening
in the Ukraine, though here it was very much more under
German influence. In the 1850s an evangelical revival occurred
among the German immigrants living in the Kherson region.
The *Mennonite Encyclopaedia* talks of 'Bible study, prayer
meetings, song festivals, evangelistic meetings, publication
efforts, conference organizations'. The primary focus of all this
was what the Germans called the *Stunde*, the 'hour' during
which small groups of believers gathered together to pray and

study the Bible. Ukrainian peasants began to appear in these groups and then later started their own. The very earliest conversion here may in fact have occurred before those in the Caucasus, but details of the movement are obscure until the emergence of Ivan Ryaboshapka, Mikhail Ratushny and Yefim Tsimbal as its leaders. Those belonging to it were originally called 'Stundists' and at a very early stage the Ukrainians began accepting baptism by immersion from their German tutors. J. G. Oncken came to carry out missionary work in this area and was a formative influence in building up these new converts into genuinely Baptist congregations.

What happened in St. Petersburg quite independently from all this was much more remarkable, because it occurred in what was then the capital city and affected several notable public figures. It all began with the illness of a child, according to Alexander Karev, the present General Secretary of the All-Union Council of Evangelical Christians and Baptists:

In the prominent family of General Chertkov, an aide-de-camp in the Tsarist army, their little boy Misha fell ill. He had come to love Christ through his tutor, an ardent Christian. Although his mother, Yelena Ivanovna Chertkova, was on the surface a very religious person, she was really a most worldly woman, but the boy strongly influenced her soul in his conversations with her. Despite all the efforts of the best doctors, Misha's condition deteriorated and finally his young eyes closed for the last time. After the child's death, his mother, who had been spiritually aroused by him, happened to meet a pious English preacher, Lord Radstock, while she was abroad (in Switzerland). She invited him to St. Petersburg and he gladly accepted the invitation.

Radstock was in fact a Plymouth Brother.[1] His preaching in the capital from March 1874 had a great influence on certain sections of the nobility, including such figures as Colonel Pashkov, Count Bobrinsky, Baron Korf and the Princesses Gagarina and Lieven. These people were all extremely affluent in a society of great inequality. Immediately an incredible development occurred: aristocrats, civil servants of all grades and ordi-

nary working people began to mix freely in the splendid homes
of the nobility for worship. Together they sang hymns, read the
Bible, said prayers and preached sermons (though usually it was
the aristocracy who did this). On one occasion over seven hundred people gathered together in the home of Colonel Pashkov.

Within the eight years between 1867–74, Protestant
doctrines had suddenly become firmly established in Russia. It
would be quite wrong for the Protestant reader in the West to
think of this as the beginning of the 'salvation' of Russia. The
Orthodox Church was still a major force in the land and—with
far-reaching modifications—remains so today. Nevertheless,
there was now a much more viable alternative to it than the
Roman Catholic Church could ever hope to be in the prevailing
political conditions. There was a new form of expression for a
personal commitment to Jesus Christ. As a modern Baptist
post-convert puts it (in a clandestine journal, *Herald of Salvation*, No. 1, 1966):

> My God
> is not an icon with its smoky lamp,
> my old mother bowing to it piously.
> That painted face is silent, stiff,
> powerless to warm the heart,
> powerless to hear my weary prayers.
>
> A man,
> crushed in the struggle,
> bends his lips and kisses it.
> But it was made by men,
> it has no life and cannot give life.
> It is dead.
> Turn, sorrowing, and leave it,
> returning to the cold crowds of the streets.
>
> My God
> is not in temples under crosses,
> incense and candles smoking,
> but where hearts burn at his touch
> and spirits burst in flame with love.

My God
is everywhere, alive in
town, village, fields, the endless woods,
capturing our hearts
and setting them free from sin.


## Baptists Grow in Adversity

These three main evangelical groups soon learned about each
other and longed for more contact, despite the huge distances
separating them. They were drawn together by a common
belief in adult baptism, despite the fact that those in St. Petersburg called themselves 'Pashkovites' (after Colonel Pashkov) or Evangelical Christians, while the other groups thought
of themselves as Baptists and Stundists respectively. For con-
venience, we refer to them all as Baptists most of the time in
this book.

Such was the vision and initiative of the St. Petersburg
Evangelical Christians that when they learned of the existence
of the others they sent out letters calling them for an informal
conference in the capital. The conveners had already, naturally
enough, aroused suspicion and hostility in the highest court
circles. They were under observation from the first, and had
even received a personal visit from K. P. Pobedonostsev, the
feared Procurator of the Holy Synod. But it was the conference
itself which brought matters to a head. Here is an account of it
from the centenary edition of the *Herald of Salvation* (No. 1,
1967), which bases itself on earlier eye-witness reports:


At the beginning of April 1884, Pashkov and Korf called a
conference in St. Petersburg of representatives of the various
strands of the movement ... Despite their different origins
and paths of development, those who met together formed
one fraternal family. A peasant sat next to a count and distinguished ladies waited upon simple people. Peasants from
Kherson, whose only equipment for the journey was the
spoon and comb which could be seen in the tops of their
boots, walked around on the shining parquet floors of the St.
Petersburg palaces. But by their decorum, humble virtue,

sincerity and piety they immediately won the hearts of their
eminent friends of the capital.

The aim of the conference was to unite all the brethren of
the Evangelical and Baptist faith, but this did not come
about. After a few days of fellowship, the participants were
arrested. The police were soon convinced that these
people—in the main, simple country folk—were not a danger
to the State, so they took them to the station and sent them
back to their homes.

In June of the same year, Pashkov and Korf were exiled
from Russia, because of their zeal in preaching the Gospel,
but at the same time I. V. Kargel returned from Bulgaria
and became the prime mover of God's work in St. Petersburg, preaching the Gospel and spiritually educating the
faithful.

These few sentences summarize the whole pattern of subsequent Russian Baptist history. The repressions at the hand of
the State became much more severe, but even at their worst
there was always someone at hand to step into the gap created
when a leader was murdered or exiled.

Pobedonostsev, despite his relatively mild treatment of those
Stundists who came to St. Petersburg for the conference,
planned to eliminate the movement altogether in the Ukraine.
The forms of worship which they used were considered to be
'crimes', so they were forced to meet secretly in the depths of
the countryside, sometimes late at night. Many were exiled.
This spread the faith to new regions, and when they returned
they immediately resumed their activities. Those whose new
loyalties became known were forced to have the word 'Stundist'
entered on their identity documents, which meant that they
were subject to all kinds of discrimination, especially where
employment was concerned. An employer who overlooked this
mark could be fined—even though these Baptist workers were
usually among the very best and never spent time in hard
drinking, nor did they seize upon the innumerable saints' days
of the Orthodox as an excuse for time off. They were not
allowed to register their marriages, so their children were
considered by the State to be illegitimate.

Documentary evidence about these persecutions was given in some pre-revolutionary Baptist publications. Here is an extract from eye-witness accounts of one series of events which occurred in the province of Yekaterinoslav (now Dnepropetrovsk). It was reprinted in the centenary edition of the *Herald of Salvation*:

We shall carry memories of November 22, 1891, with us to the grave. On the morning of that day people began to congregate in our village from all the neighbouring settlements and hamlets. Some came in waggons, others on sledges (for there was already snow). There were police on foot and horseback. We were surprised and started to ask what was going on. "They're going to take away the Stundists' children," they told us. A commotion began in the houses of all believers where there were children. They arrested us—Grigori Cherdak, Yevstakhi Likhograi, Grigori Volochai and others—and sent us to the village administration office . . .

"Now, you Stundists," began the priest (who had been waiting for them), "up to now, as your pastors, we've been using words to persuade you to return to Orthodoxy, but from here on we'll do it by the force of authority. We've received a circular from the governor which states: 'Reconvert the Stundists, using every means to do so.' Now you must give us a signature that you're returning to the Orthodox Church. Anyone who doesn't comply will have his children taken away. Sign!" But not a single one of us agreed. "Go on", said the priest to the police. We already knew where he was sending them, but couldn't do anything, for we were under guard . . .

A turmoil began throughout the village. A crowd of people with sticks in their hands, accompanied by police, went in turn to all the houses where there were Baptists and took away the children, giving them to anyone who wanted to take them. The children screamed and ran bare-footed through the snow from one street to another. They hid themselves in hayricks, but they were found, put on to a sledge and taken to the village administration office, where the police sorted out who was to take whom.

The children of my husband's brother ran to us, bare-footed and unclad, for their uncle to protect them. There was a crowd chasing them. My husband let the children into the hut, but went out himself to face the people. "Sign your agreement that you're returning to the Orthodox Church," said the village policeman. My husband refused. Then the policeman demanded the children. "I won't give them up", said my husband, and called out to me, "Shut the door!" I did so and put the hook down, while he stood outside the door to stop people breaking it down. But they knocked him off his feet at once, tied up his hands and just left him lying on the ground.

"Open up!" shouted the policeman to me. "I shan't!" I replied, seizing hold of the hook with my hand. "Break down the doors!" screamed the policeman. They shuddered, the hook shattered and several men burst into the hut shouting. I was trembling with fear. "Where are the children?" asked the policeman. "You'd better look for them," I replied. They searched high and low, but didn't find them. "Where have you hidden them?" they cried and started to assault me.

The children knew that the people had come to take them away and had hidden themselves under the stove and in the attic. I could see that there was nothing to be done and that they would have to be given up, so I started to call them. They wept and wouldn't leave. I had great difficulty in per-suading them, but finally gathered them together and took them to the policeman . . .

They took three boys of nine, seven and two years old from Grigori Kuchugurny and handed them over to some-one—I don't remember who it was—in the village of Tar-asovka. Kuchugurny's wife Daria was ill at that time and when they came to take the children she was lying in bed with her two-year-old son. For a long time she wouldn't give him up, but they tore him away from her arms. After that she got even worse and died two weeks later . . .

After a month an order came from the governor that the children should be returned. This was done, but God alone knows what the mothers went through during that time.

The life of Vasili Pavlov very well sums up the tribulations and unflinching faith of the earliest Russian Baptists, the corner-stone upon which the later development of the faith was founded. We are especially fortunate in knowing his biography in some detail, for he left a memoir which in 1965 was given prominence again by the *Herald of Salvation*. Here are a few short extracts from *Memoirs of an Exile:*

MY CONVERSION

By God's grace I was brought to a realization of my sinful state and to a sincere belief in Christ when I was sixteen . . .

My parents were Molokans, members of a sect which very closely resembles the Protestant faith but, like the Quakers, they deny baptism and the Lord's Supper. Through reading the New Testament and talking with Baptists, I became convinced that I must be baptized. In 1870 I joined the Baptist congregation in Tiflis (in the Caucasus), which had only just been formed and which consisted of no more than a handful of people. My parents were against this and I had to suffer for it even at that time. Gradually, however, they, too, started to be convinced by these teachings of Christ and they began to visit our meetings.

Despite my youth, I tried to attract others to the Lord and sometimes the brethren made me read God's Word and expound it at the meeting . . .

ARREST AND SECOND EXILE

One morning while we were still sleeping, the village elder knocked at the door of my house and invited me to go to the police officer. The latter announced that the Governor of Tiflis had ordered my arrest. I was to go to Tiflis, so that from there I could be sent to Orenburg again[2] under the vigilance of the police for four years. I took this news home and told my wife who was naturally utterly downcast. This was August 5, 1891.

So I was arrested. They kept watch on us while we gathered up our things and I hired a horse and cart to take us to Tiflis . . . I spent the night in a police cell on a bare plank bed in my summer clothes.

T—B

The next day my wife and the brethren found me with difficulty and brought me food, but no one was allowed to speak to me. However, one of the guards here was an acquaintance of mine. Another policeman had a Bible and we discussed the faith together.

... Finally, early in the morning of September 16 we reached Orenburg, where I spent one day in the prison and was then released.

ORENBURG AGAIN

When I arrived in Orenburg, I moved into a friend's basement room. My family remained in Tiflis for the winter, for it is much colder in Orenburg, where the thermometer falls to −40°. Already in October it was bitterly cold.

As soon as I arrived here, my friends were overjoyed and during October I baptized several people, because the soil had already been prepared ...

Golovkin, an Orthodox missionary, sought me out in my hut, talked with me about the truths of the faith, and then told me that Bishop Makari would like to converse with me.

On December 3 the missionary and I visited the bishop. He received me kindly, enquired about my situation, my family, and so on. I told him that I was in my second spell of exile here. He said he would like me to debate publicly with Golovkin. I willingly agreed to this, provided the authorities should approve.

ARRIVAL AND DEATH OF MY FAMILY

... Finally at the end of March 1892 my wife and five children arrived ... but we were not destined to live long together.

The whole population was seriously affected by famine. The government distributed relief to the people in corn. The brethren from St. Petersburg sent one waggon-load of maize flour, which I distributed to our fellow-believers.

In July two of my children fell ill—my daughter Nadezhda and the infant Misha. I sent them into the nearest village,

Blagoslovenka, about eight miles from Orenburg, while I
had to stay on in the town, because I could not move without
special permission.

[Shortly after this, Pavlov's twelve-year-old daughter was acci-
dentally drowned.]

At that time cholera was already raging in the town and
we decided to be all together, so that if anyone should die, it
would happen in each other's presence. In the evenings
Muslims, Jews, Orthodox and Old Believers would all
process around the streets beseeching God for mercy and the
end of the epidemic. The town became sober, for shouting,
songs and drunkenness were to be heard no more in the
taverns. Orenburg was like penitent Nineveh—but how soon
all that ended! Wherever you went, you would come upon
coffins with corpses. Our neighbours were dying from cholera
and we prepared ourselves to meet the same fate.

On July 26, a Sunday, we were well when we got up in the
morning and drank tea. My wife and elder daughter then
began to complain of a headache. My wife became worse and
I called the doctor. He found no evidence of cholera, but
prescribed a preventive medicine, just in case, and I went
round to the chemist's for it. After lunch the children started
to have diarrhoea and everyone became worse. I harnessed
the horse and cart and took them out to the fresh air in the
woods. But this was of no avail. Finally my wife started to
have convulsions and I hastened to take them home. There
was no doubt that death was casting its black shadow on our
family. I summoned another doctor. He shook his head and
advised everyone to go to the hospital, for I would be able to
do nothing for them on my own. I objected that I could not
entrust them to the care of others, since the hospitals were
filled to overflowing. He replied that I could tend them
myself in hospital . . .

They were all in the grip of a dreadful fever, except the
infant, who was showing no signs of cholera. At midnight my
wife's lips stopped moving and she left this world. By
Monday morning my second son, Peter, aged six, had fol-

lowed his mother. That day a cart loaded with coffins received two more, containing the bodies of two people who had been so dear to me. I followed them alone on a horse-drawn sled and watched how they were buried in the earth. The sisters Zhivult arrived only at the end of the interment.

But it was already time to hurry back to those who were still alive, though struggling with death. Finally, on July 30, two more children were carried off, my elder daughter Vera and the infant Misha (one-and-a-half). Vera died fully conscious and I prayed with her, commending her to the Saviour. These children were buried in the same way.

In the hospital yard carpenters hardly had time to make the coffins. Corpses were being removed dozens at a time to make way for new patients. Very, very few recovered. I was in the valley of the shadow of death, but the Lord was with me. I asked myself why I should be still alive when all my dear ones had been taken away. But an inner voice said: "There is still a purpose in life. Live for Jesus who has redeemed you." I called to mind, "For whether we live, we live unto the Lord; and whether we die, we die unto the Lord."

I still had one son remaining alive—Paul, aged nine. He was hardly breathing, but the doctors assured me that he would not die. I remained with him until Saturday, when the doctor told me to take him home.

I left the hospital, but alas, how empty our house seemed! Everything was in its place, but the owners had departed, leaving the two of us to wander here alone! The Lord had mercy on me and in about two weeks Paul gradually improved.

Soon my father came from the Caucasus, but he found only one of his grandsons. While my family was with me, my exile had not been so unbearable. In October Pastors Chetverkin and Balikhin came to visit me, having undertaken a great journey to console me.

These few pages illustrate graphically the fearful sufferings of a Baptist leader in the early days of the new Church's life in Russia. The cholera epidemic was, of course, a natural disaster outside the control of the Tsarist authorities, though bad living conditions resulting from enforced exile aggravated it. Their inhumanity in not allowing Pavlov to leave Orenburg for the surrounding countryside comes out clearly in the memoirs. What a contrast to the humanity of the religious believers of different religions who made a common cause to pray for deliverance and of the pastors who came right out to the Urals to visit their bereaved brother!

Then, as now, it was precisely where conditions were least human that the faith took firmest root.


## The End of the Tsarist Era

At the beginning of the twentieth century the situation improved. In 1903–4 there were edicts proclaiming tolerance (by this time the last Tsar, Nicholas II, was prepared to make concessions on many fronts in his anxiety to remain in power). It was now no longer a crime to leave the Orthodox Church. Children were allowed to go to school without being forced to attend lessons on the Orthodox catechism, which had formerly been obligatory. After the social disturbances of the 1905 revolution the boundaries of freedom were considerably widened. Large numbers of exiles returned and there were even possibilities of organizing missionary work.

The first such society was founded at Rostov-on-Don in May 1907. Apart from local preachers already there, fifty evangelists moved into the area. They set up Sunday schools and discussion groups for young people. In 1909 a Baptist congress was held there and it established the 'All-Russian Union of Baptist Youth Circles'. With a tradition like this in Rostov, it is not surprising to find it in the news again today because of the evangelistic activities of its students, which have been criticized in the Soviet press. Pastors' conferences were held in other places, too, and these men placed particular emphasis on the need for the religious education of young people. These years after 1905 also saw the establishment of a considerable Baptist publishing activity. Journals such as *The Christian, The Baptist, The Good News, Friend of Youth* and *Rainbow* were all founded then. Hymn books, Bibles and concordances were also published.

Despite these improvements, which led to a rapid growth of Baptist membership, the 'liberalization' had hardly begun before new fears and tensions developed. The documents of the time demonstrate most impressively the concern of Baptist leaders for a full legal guarantee of their rights—a concern which has been repeated in more difficult circumstances but with equal objectivity since 1961. At a congress in 1910 the Latvian Baptist missionary, William Fetler, spoke as follows:

Freedom of conscience has been given us, but the local administration subjects Baptists to all sorts of repressions. Our congregations are refused registration and are not allowed to pray. It is essential to ask the Ministry to issue one general circular for the whole of Russia, in which it is clearly and precisely set out what we Baptists may and may not do.

The law on sectarian congregations contradicts the demands of our Baptist beliefs. It does not allow us to receive young people of fourteen to twenty-one into our midst and to baptize them. Our Saviour said: 'Go ye therefore, and teach all nations', but he did not set any age-limit. He demanded only a conscious acceptance of faith and repentance. Therefore if a man turns to the Lord he must be baptized.

The law on sectarian congregations is incomplete. It talks of individual congregations, but does not envisage a union of them. In fact such a union does exist and we cannot live without it, but it is vital to petition for its recognition as a legal entity.

Fifty years later, each of those points is still a controversial and painful issue. The name of the oppressor changes, but the methods of oppression are remarkably consistent. Registration of congregations was a Tsarist invention taken over into Stalin's body of laws on religion codified in 1929. Before the Revolution people were deprived of the right to worship because the authorities would not register the congregations to which they belonged. The same thing is true today. One wonders whether Fetler foresaw that sixty years later it would be a crime punishable by three years' imprisonment to baptize a young person under eighteen (though infant baptism is permitted to the children of those Orthodox parents who risk demanding it); or that the congregation would still be denied the legal right to take any corporate action—it has no right to meet for any purposes whatsoever, except in the context of worship. Special permission must be given for any other meeting, which is granted only in the rarest instances.

Between Fetler's speech and the Revolution of 1917 things became worse instead of better. This incident occurred at the village of Vasilkova, also in the province of Yekaterinoslav, in 1914, and the description is taken from a Baptist calendar of that year, *The Good Counsellor*:

On May 19 all the members of the congregation were to assemble for common prayer. Some feared an attack from Rakhno [an Orthodox peasant who had been threatening to break up their meetings], but V. P. Kisil, as a good pastor should, consoled the timid with the words of Christ: "Are not two sparrows sold for a farthing? And one of them shall not fall to the ground without your Father." He himself led the way into the meeting ...

Rakhno entered the prayer house and cried out to Kisil, "Stand up, get out!" The innocent victim stood up without uttering a word, just like a silent lamb. Then the murderer threw himself at him and did his bloodthirsty and brutal deed, running a dagger right into his heart. It was all over in a second. After his criminal act, he was the first to dash out of the prayerhouse and off to the Orthodox Church where, according to rumour, he proclaimed that he had destroyed one of the enemy. He wiped his bloody hands in the porch, where he was arrested.

We may say of our dear late Brother Kisil, "He was true unto death; he has fought a good fight, he has finished his course, he has kept the faith. Henceforth there is laid up for him a crown of righteousness, which the Lord, the righteous judge, shall give him at that day. His memory will not be erased from among us."

Pastor Bukreyev, a friend and fellow-worker of the dead

man, writes thus: "This is a terrible deed which is hard to bear. It reminds us of the years of the bloody repression of the Stundists during the régime of Pobedonostsev. It is appalling to think that among Orthodox Christians there could be a fanatic who would lift his hand against the pastor of a Christian congregation in a place where the Word of God is read and prayers are offered. The fact is no less terrible that apparently other people were mixed up in this business, who were using Rakhno as a blind tool.

"What makes this evil even worse is the fact that in telegrams which have been despatched around Russia the murder is ascribed to the sectarians themselves. Who could perpetrate such a lie?

"This reminds us of those times gone by. In one place they routed the Stundists and then brought the Stundists themselves to court for having caused the pogrom. Is it not true that, even though homage is being paid to religious freedom, sectarians are even now like lambs brought to the slaughter?"

It would not, of course, be wise to generalize from an isolated incident and state that persecutions were as bad just before the Revolution as at the end of the nineteenth century. Equally today it would also be a misrepresentation to interpret the deeds of isolated maniacs and sadists as expressions of official policy. The point, however, in all these instances is that there are not enough safeguards against such events; indeed, one could say that a climate of opinion is encouraged in which such things are always likely to happen. Even today Baptists are calculatedly accused of foul crimes which they did not commit. The present-day Russian Baptist leadership is quite correct when it states that its forerunners never knew true freedom before the Communist Revolution. The question which will concern us from here on is whether they ever knew it later.

## NOTES

1. Now known as the 'Open' or Christian Brethren.
2. This was the place of Pavlov's first exile.

*Chapter III*

# LIFE UNDER STALIN

*A Golden Decade*

The abdication of the Russian Tsar and the accession to power of the Provisional Government in March 1917 brought about a dramatic change for the better in the life of the Russian Baptists. On March 16 it was decreed that 'all social, religious and national restrictions' should be abolished and that there should be 'an immediate general amnesty for all political and religious offences'. Baptists who had been in prison and exile streamed homewards and many attempted to take up the threads of their normal lives which had been severed years earlier.

It cannot be said, however, that even now the Baptists achieved complete religious equality. The Russian Orthodox Church remained in a position of entrenched privilege, despite the loss of its parochial schools. It still commanded a considerable state subsidy, probably because the new government did not want to alienate such an influential body. At the same time, in the conditions of near-chaos which gripped the country, Baptists had full personal freedom to preach the gospel where and when they wished. As a prominent evangelist of those days put it: "The country became one big auditorium, with innumerable meetings everywhere . . . On the streets of the cities, in the parks, in public halls, in theatres, at railway stations, on trains, on board ships, in factories—everywhere one could hear the singing of gospel hymns and good evangelical preaching." In the whole history of the Russian Baptist movement it is doubtful if this could have been true of any other six-month period. It was a Prague spring of the early twentieth century.

There were other new developments during those days, too.

According to Vasili Pavlov, tens of thousands of Russian prisoners of war came into contact with Evangelical Christians in
Germany. Thousands were converted and hundreds received instruction from the Bible. When these men returned home they
became 'a source from which a great stream of blessings'
flowed through the land of Russia, as a Russian Baptist writer
put it.

The All-Russian Union of Evangelical Christians, with its
aristocratic and intellectual background in the capital, became
more involved in politics at this time. Its leaders put forward a
programme in which they claimed that in these days of great
instability and uncertainty their type of Christian faith held the
greatest hope of salvation for Russia. They proposed that the
Orthodox Church should be disestablished and that the primacy of the local congregation should be recovered. All religions and denominations should have complete equality
before the law and they should be allowed to arrange any meetings or congresses at will. Societies should be formed which
would promote evangelical principles by popularizing Christ's
teachings and combating such common vices as alcoholism.
The Protestant denominations were also in the forefront of the
desire for peace which had swept through Russia by the middle
of 1917, that fourth weary year of the struggle with Germany.

When the Communist Party came to power as a result of the
Revolution of October 1917, one of the earliest measures taken
by Lenin was to call for separation of Church and State. This
he did in his decree of January 23, 1918. Despite the new law's
insistence on freedom of conscience, the Russian Orthodox
Church very rapidly discovered that the new decree could be
used as a pretext for religious persecution. Being so closely
identified with the old régime was a severe handicap. One
result of it was a nationwide campaign to root out the Orthodox
Church from all positions of influence in society.

This identification with the past did not, of course, apply to
the Russian Baptists. Rather the opposite. As a group which
had been seriously persecuted by both the Tsarist authorities
and the Orthodox Church, the Baptists found themselves in
1917 at the beginning of a decade of special privilege. They

were less molested during the next ten years than in any other comparable period in their hundred-year history.

One of the guarantees in Lenin's new religious law was of 'freedom for religious and anti-religious propaganda to all citizens'. Although this provision lasted on the statute book for little over a decade, the Baptists, unlike the Orthodox, were able to make good use of it while it was there. For them it was a time of missionary expansion, with new enterprises growing up in several remote parts of Siberia, in Central Asia, the Far East, the Western Ukraine and Belorussia. P. V. Ivanov-Klyshnikov, one of the foremost evangelists of the time, adopted as his slogan, 'Christ for the heathen and the Muslims in the U.S.S.R.' This evangelistic zeal, allied to a concern for all the various ethnic and religious communities in the nation, has been a distinctively Baptist trait right up to the present. It has enabled them to cut right across the prevalent notion that a Central Asian may be Muslim, but a Russian must be Orthodox.

In the mid-1920s Bible courses were organized in Leningrad for the training of preachers. Despite the scarcity of paper, it is significant that some of the Protestant publishing activity which had been such a feature of the early years of the century was resumed, having ceased during the time of the First World War and the Revolution. *The Christian* was resumed in 1924 and *The Baptist* in 1925, while a new *Baptist of the Ukraine* was founded in 1926.

The Evangelical Christians were especially active in this publishing movement. Bibles were printed in Leningrad and Kiev, while there were also editions of the New Testament, a concordance and two hymn books (*The Voice of Truth* and *The Harp*)—including music editions.

The most notable advance of all, however, was in Christian instruction. Meetings were held to discuss suitable methods and programmes. In many congregations there were activity groups for women and young people, designed to bring together persons of common interests under the auspices of the Church.

The leading light among the Baptists at this time was Ivan Stepanovich Prokhanov, who had first of all come into prominence under the Tsarist régime. He was a man versed in the sciences as well as in theology. He represented the American firm of Westinghouse and this took him throughout Russia, enabling him to build up a wide range of contacts before the Revolution. His great aim, both before and after 1917, was to combine his knowledge of architecture and planning with his religious convictions in order to set up a completely Christian township or commune.

The new régime itself wanted to establish new economic units in underdeveloped areas and at first assented to Prokhanov's plans. After a considerable search, he found an ideal site in the Altai province at the confluence between the rivers Biya and Katun. Here he would found 'Evangelsk', the 'City of the Gospel' (some called it 'City of the Sun').

On September 11, 1927, a unique event occurred. Two representatives of the Evangelical Christians, together with a number of local communist officials, went out together for a formal tree-planting ceremony. Young oaks were chosen—they would grow into sturdy trees and become a visual symbol of the new Russia. The Evangelical journal, *The Christian*, in its first issue of 1928 gave an account of the plans for the project, with considerable architectural details designed to aid both agricultural prosperity and a full religious life. There would be a large round central open space over a mile in diameter, from which the streets would radiate like sunbeams. All the imposing buildings in between the streets—hospitals, church schools, places of worship, dwellings—would be laid out among beautiful parks with variegated trees.

Prokhanov intended to finance his project with funds from abroad—especially from America. With his contacts he very likely would have been successful in raising the vast sum of money required. But his plans never went beyond the drawing-board. That issue of *The Christian*, however, remains a unique piece of printed literature in the Soviet Union. Its publication was soon to be followed by the Soviet drive for collectivization in earnest. The Communist Party came to fear Prokhanov's plans not only because of their religious basis, but also because they might well have been successful. The new ideologists would have been discredited if it could have been seen that only people with a non-Communist faith could construct successful communes.

Prokhanov was driven out, to die in exile in Berlin in 1935. No one in the Soviet Union has ever thought like him since.

## Back to the Catacombs

Lenin died in 1924. His successor was Stalin. The Baptists' freedom lasted as long as it took Stalin to gather the reins of power firmly into his hands. Within a year or two he was totally committed to the programme of industrialization, enforced collectivization and the elimination of every element in society which he regarded as a potential threat to his person or his programme. The persecution of religion had begun in earnest.

Publishing came to a peremptory halt. The Bible School in Leningrad closed its doors in 1928, to be 'reopened as a correspondence course after a certain interval', as Alexander Karev later rather quaintly phrased it—glossing over a mere forty years, or nearly half of Baptist history in Russia at the time he spoke!

From the legal point of view, the most catastrophic event in the life of the churches at this time was the promulgation of Stalin's 'Law on Religious Associations' of 1929. It is a most odd piece of legislation. If the Soviet Union had a legal profession whose livelihood depended on interpreting the laws objectively (which it has not) these sixty-eight provisions would cause them many headaches. This law gives a recipe for obstruction and bureaucratic frustration. It tells a church, as a religious body, almost nothing of what it may do, but lists in detail what it may *not* do—and these prohibitions have remained almost unchanged for forty years. If anything, they have since been tightened in certain respects.

In the West we accept without question the right to bring up our children to follow our own religious convictions. We accept that often in later life they go their own ways, but we nevertheless consider that the grounding in Christian morality which we are able to give them ourselves, or which is given them by the teachers in the school we select for our children, will be of value in establishing their standards and attitudes. These remarks apply to Britain, where religion is compulsory in state schools (except where parents contract their children out of this subject), as well as to the United States (where religion is not taught in the public schools, but where parents have the full right to choose a church school, if they wish).

What of the Soviet Union? The legal situation there is that the organized teaching of religion to anyone under eighteen is illegal and punishable by a prison sentence of up to three years. This penalty has frequently been invoked for people who have organized Sunday schools quite informally by gathering a few children together in each other's homes. Even a parent who teaches religion to his own children privately with no outsiders present is in danger of having the child removed and sent to a boarding school, where he will be given a Soviet education away from the influence of 'religious fanaticism'. The only sort of religious education which is allowed in practice is theological training for those over eighteen who manage to gain entrance to one of the handful of seminaries (Orthodox, Catholic, Armenian or Georgian) which still function. Even this was not permitted until after the Second World War. Discounting such things as Bible correspondence courses, which have operated sporadically for Baptists, Lutherans and others, there are probably not more than about five hundred students of all denominations undergoing theological education in the whole Soviet Union today. There are many more Roman Catholic students in New York State alone. Some denominations (for example, Seventh-Day Adventists, Eastern-Rite Catholics, Methodists, Mennonites) are allowed no theological education of any description—the Eastern-Rite Catholics are even denied legal existence.

If these severe restrictions were the whole story, the situation would be bad, but not quite so serious as it in fact is. Alongside the absence of religious education, there is the universal presence of compulsory atheist education. This does not stem from the 1929 law, but from Communist Party decrees. No parent has the right of contracting a child out of the compulsory atheistic instruction which is in the school curriculum. This goes right on into the university system. In 1964 there was a decree placing more emphasis on atheism throughout the higher education establishments—and it was to be a compulsory subject, without proficiency in which it would be most difficult to complete the course in one's main subjects. Even a student who has decided to become a priest or a pastor while at school is forced to attend lessons in atheism.

It does not take much imagination to appreciate that this enforced teaching of atheism can often result in the most severe psychological conflicts in a child, where parents at home try to erase the effects of the scorn which has been poured on his faith and that of his parents during his instruction from the teacher. Yet, wherever such conflicts have arisen—and they have probably been more acute in recent years since the State began to pay increased attention to atheism in education—the blame for this tension has invariably been laid on the parents.

A further clause which is basic to the 1929 law and which has been consistently discriminatory against believers is that of registration. The law states that in order to worship legally, a group of at least twenty believers of the same faith (be they Baptists, Orthodox, Muslims or Jews) must petition the local authorities for permission to register as a 'religious society' (to use the Soviet term). If the application is approved by the local authorities, it is forwarded through a complex bureaucratic system until it eventually reaches the Council for Religious Affairs (as the appropriate government body is now called) in Moscow. Only when central approval has been confirmed is the body considered registered and therefore legal. Any activity undertaken in the interim (for example, worship or prayer meetings) is considered illegal and is severely punishable under the law.

When registration is approved, then a building is provided by the State for religious worship. Naturally, this system gives immense scope not only for long periods of delay, during which the applying body remains in suspension or a sort of penumbra, but also for complete refusal of registration. Despite the basic concept in the law, therefore, of the separation of Church and State, there is built into the system absolute and direct control by the secular authorities of the activities of the religious community. When one adds to this the fact that in practice the priest or pastor has also to be personally 'registered', the degree of control is very considerable. Indeed, legal discrimination is so acute that without a certain amount of good will on the part of the local authorities, no religious activities at all are legally possible within the community. No registration—no church—illegal religious activity: this is the syndrome which has governed the lives of thousands of would-be Christian communities in the Soviet Union since the establishment of Stalinist power.

Even where communities have legally registered, this is still no guarantee that they will be able to carry on their activities unmolested. Rather the contrary. Not only have they guaranteed to abide by all the clauses of the law which discriminates against them before they can be registered at all; much more seriously, there is the notorious Paragraph 14 of the 1929 law. This states that the church community, once it is legally formed, exists under the guidance of an executive committee of three people. Any member of this triumvirate may be removed, the law states, at the pleasure of the local communist authorities. The inevitable consequence is that most communities are not under the guidance of their most competent organizers or their most dedicated believers: such people are simply prevented from reaching any office without any reason being given. There are even known instances where the communists have been able to insinuate their own people into key positions in the local religious community and the law has protected them from recrimination. This is like a battle in which one army can appoint its own men to key positions on the other side, and is without doubt the most dangerous threat to Christian activity in the Soviet Union today. Although its implementation has not been consistent, Stalin's law placed the Church under the rigorous control of the communist authorities.

A further form of control which particularly affects Christians of the Protestant tradition is that evangelism is strictly limited to the building which has been registered for worship. This means that the whole superstructure of additional activities, so normal for Protestant (and indeed Catholic) churches in western Europe and America, is totally impossible in the Soviet Union. It is not even legal for a pastor to preach in a church other than his own, let alone carry on any other form of evangelism.

The printing of literature, too, is strictly under the control of the State. Throughout the 1930's the Churches could produce no Christian literature whatsoever; since the Second World War the Baptists have been permitted six issues of *Fraternal Messenger* a year, the Russian Orthodox a monthly *Journal of the Moscow Patriarchate*. Bibles and hymn books have been produced in minute editions which do not even begin to meet the needs. It is claimed that 20,000 Bibles have recently been printed for the Baptists, but it is not known how many have reached the congregations. Beyond that, there has been nothing other than an occasional book for the Russian Orthodox Church, apparently published mainly for its foreign propaganda value to the Soviet Government.

Even where the 1929 law seems to offer a small loophole of freedom to the Church, it is not all it seems to be. For example, it is stated that a priest or pastor may visit hospital in order to minister to the 'religious needs' of the sick. However, there is, as usual, a qualifying clause—that such religious rites must be carried out in a separate room (so as not to 'contaminate' other patients, one presumes). Anyone who has ever visited a Soviet hospital will know how ludicrous this provision is. The overcrowding is unbelievable, with scarcely space to walk between the beds. Private ward or room for a Christian? The idea has a touch of surrealism about it that may even have been intended by the maker of the law.

Reviewing the legal position of the churches in the Soviet Union and the system laid down by Stalin which has been so little modified in the last forty years, one is forced to the conclusion that there is no other country in the world, apart from Albania and China, where more discrimination against Christians is written into the statute book. Anything comparable written against the black people of America would have long since caused a major armed uprising. In Albania and China religion, it appears, has now been legally abolished, so the Church there is forced to lead an entirely underground existence. So far, the Soviet Union has never approached this extreme point, but it is still committed, on the repeated assurance of its leaders, to an eventual total eradication of all forms of religion.

So after the 'golden decade' for the Russian Baptists which followed the Revolution, there then came the 1929 law. It introduced, as intended, a period of the most intense persecution, far more brutal and all-embracing than anything which had taken place under the Tsars. Of course, many other sections of Soviet society, not least the Communist Party itself, were grievously affected during the period of the Great Purges. The Baptists were not singled out as an especially undesirable element in society, in the way that many of the most active have been since 1960. Nevertheless, the temporary hopes which many had entertained were now permanently dashed.

Let us look at the sudden decline in the fortunes of the Russian Baptists, as experienced by one man, Nikolai Odintsov. Here is an extract from a memoir of him as written by an anonymous young Baptist and published clandestinely in the *Herald of Salvation* in 1964:

On December 11, 1927, Brother Nikolai Odintsov arrived at Khabarovsk, where he was met by local believers who had come to the railway station. Brother Nikolai went straight from the station to the meeting, where the brothers and sisters of the Khabarovsk congregation, especially the young people, gave an ecstatic welcome to the dear guest from Moscow. When the doors of the church opened and the thick-set figure of Brother Nikolai appeared, a wave of intense excitement passed over the assembled congregation. They rejoiced and thanked God for the safe arrival of the dear guest.

Brother Odintsov visited the believers at Vladivostok, Blagoveshchensk and other places. This was indeed a missionary journey. The brother saw with his own eyes that God's work was successfully developing not only at the centre, but also at the periphery, not only in warm climes, but also among the woods, in the hostile *taiga* and in the far East.

1928 arrives—the summit of Nikolai Odintsov's spiritual activity, his apogee. He was in his fifty-eighth year. He went to the fifth All-Ukrainian Baptist Congress in Kharkov, which took place from May 10–31, 1928. At one of its sessions there was a report on the losses which the Baptist Union had suffered, especially in connection with the murder of Brother Kandelaki, a Georgian by nationality, who fell fighting on the spiritual battleground on August 24, 1927. Brother Odintsov was deeply affected by the loss of one of the most zealous and ardent workers. In the conference hall the delegates with tears in their eyes sang the hymn, 'We are at the earthly shore'.

The Fourth World Baptist Congress was held at Toronto (Canada) from June 23–30, 1928 ... Brother Odintsov headed the Russian delegation of eleven and pronounced a short speech of greeting in the name of the Russian Baptists.

But already at this time clouds of repression and persecution were hanging over Christians and threatening them for their faith in God. Odintsov's last published work was an article printed in *The Baptist* (No. 2 of 1929) ... One could say of Brother Odintsov that he, too, was a model for the faithful. His whole life belonged to the Lord and he strove to fulfil His will with an absolute submission. He was a good preceptor of children and young people, of the brethren and of the preachers of the Gospel, and in general of all the servants of God. He desired that believers should hold high the banner of spiritual struggle.

He gave a message of encouragement to believers from the chair of the 22nd Congress of Siberian Baptists: "I would wish you to hold high the banner of our exalted service to the Lord. Give sincere and heartfelt greetings to all the brothers and sisters whom I dearly love."

[In the autumn of 1933 Nikolai Odintsov was arrested.]

I never set eyes on Brother Nikolai and did not know him personally. In my childhood and youth I dreamed only of meeting him face to face on this earth, but my dreams were not destined to be fulfilled.

In 1939, when I first came to Moscow, I visited the house

outside the city where Brother Odintsov lived until his arrest. There I met his wife, Alexandra Stepanova Odintsova, who was by then an old lady, an ardent Christian, who had lost her husband for the sake of Christ and His Gospel.

Alexandra Odintsova recounted that after 1933 her husband sent to her in his letters a whole series of sermons which were full of consolation and encouragement. Finally in 1937 they allowed her to meet him. She went to see him in distant Siberia. He was exhausted and physically weak, but full of faith in the Almighty. The tears of the dear brother were not tears of despair, but of a weak body. He was sixty-seven years old by now and the conditions of his confinement had been severe. Their time together did not last long. They soon removed her husband and Alexandra never received any further news of him.

After the war some believers testified in Moscow that Brother Odintsov had been eaten alive by dogs which the escorts set on him during his transfer to the Krasnoyarsk region in 1939 . . .

So he departed from us without a farewell greeting, without a valedictory letter and without leaving us any spiritual testimony. He fulfilled the course of his life in obscurity.

Brother Odintsov's wife remembers her thoughts about him when he was still the president of the Federated Union of Baptists. At that time she was enthralled by his tireless activity and thought that if he should die *The Baptist* would be entirely filled with laudatory articles about his deeds and that people in the farthest corners of the land would know about his funeral. However, "There are many devices in a man's heart; nevertheless the counsel of the Lord, that shall stand" (Proverbs 19:21). Instead of fame to the farthest corners of the land, Brother Odintsov perished in complete anonymity; instead of laurel wreaths he had briers and thorns, barbed wire and a martyr's death. Though he is no longer on earth, I do not know where his grave is. Did he have one at all? However, I imagine to myself his kind face and say, "Farewell, until we meet in heaven in the solemnity of the future resurrection."

The list of heroes of the faith given in Chapter 11 of the Epistle to the Hebrews may be extended to include the name of Nikolai Odintsov.

This pathetic memoir illustrates the catastrophic decline in the fortunes of the Russian Baptists in the 1930s. From a situation of promise, where it seemed that at last the life of the Russian Baptists might settle down to a reasonable degree of normality, a whole generation of its leaders was swept away. The only 'normality' was continuing persecution. Although the Baptists kept going as an undergound Church, it was no longer possible to talk of them as an organization. Not all their leaders suffered the martyr's death of Nikolai Odintsov, but those who escaped it languished in prisons and camps in comparable obscurity.

Almost all the recent leaders of the All-Union Council of Evangelical Christians and Baptists in Moscow went to prison at this time. The only one who is known to have remained free was Mikhail Orlov, who died in 1961 and whose son is now an official of the Moscow Baptist church, speaks English well and is known to many foreign visitors.

What of those leaders who went to prison, submerged in the swirling and terrifying sea of Stalin's purges, but somehow managed to pull through alive? A further trick of fate awaited them—though the precise details of what happened remain the greatest mystery in the history of the Russian Baptists.

In 1941 the Soviet Union was engulfed in World War II, having at first trusted Hitler and signed a pact with him, and then suffered an ignominious rebuff when the Germans invaded Russia. These events were of little immediate significance for most of the millions of political prisoners, except that the food shortage became even more acute than it had been before.

In the Kremlin, however, Stalin was reconsidering his policy towards religion—not as a calculated act of goodwill, but in a desperate attempt to rally all sectors of opinion in the country behind the war effort. Such morale as existed in the country after the Revolution had been shattered by the purges which had eliminated most of the intellectuals and even most of the

ablest men in the Communist Party itself. The enforced collectivization of agriculture (which sapped the morale of the
peasants, who felt they were being submerged into vast communes) and the sudden shock of the German invasion threatened a national collapse before battle had even been properly
joined. Stalin's only possible recourse was to appeal to patri-
otism—and that entailed making concessions to the Russian
Orthodox Church to enable it to re-establish the basic organization of its life. This was recognized in 1943, when the three
leading Orthodox figures at liberty were received by Stalin in
the Kremlin and immediately afterwards Metropolitan Sergius
was elected Patriarch—a position which had been vacant for
nearly twenty years.

The substance of that conversation in the Kremlin has never
been revealed by either the Church or the State. We know
nothing of the nature of the bargaining, the details of the concessions Stalin made, or the price he demanded for them. We
know only the outward results: that soon after this the Russian
Orthodox Church was able to open eight theological seminaries, to consecrate bishops, to re-open parishes and to resume
publication of the monthly *Journal of the Moscow Patriarchate*.

For the Baptists we have even fewer details of what actually
occurred in the negotiations with the government. But the fact is
that they achieved in 1944 what they had unsuccessfully tried
to bring about at that ill-fated congress in St. Petersburg in
1883—a union between the Baptist and the Evangelical Christian wings of the Protestant church in the Soviet Union. The
name for the body which was to control this new united Church
was 'The All-Union Council of Evangelical Christians and
Baptists' (later the 'and' was replaced by a hyphen, supposedly
to emphasize symbolically the unity which had been achieved).
Clearly the formal status of the Protestants was improved
through the merger of the separate administrative bodies of
Evangelical Christians and Baptists—bodies which had in any
case been dissolved during the 1930s. Like the Orthodox, the
Baptists managed to begin publishing a journal—*The Fraternal
Herald*, which, in this instance, was to appear every other
month. Though no gains were made in the field of religious

education, it soon became possible to legalize congregations
through registering them. People always tend to turn towards
religion during times of war, which benefited all religious denominations in the Soviet Union at this time.

The mystery which we have mentioned lies just here: what
was the exact nature of this controlling body, the All-Union
Council? What were its real relations with the State? What sort
of compromises had it to make to achieve these concessions
from the authorities? To what extent did it truly represent the
interests and wishes of the Evangelical Christians and Baptists
of the land?

Such answers as we can glean to these questions are disturbing. Here, for example, is a report on these events written
in 1963 by Gennadi Kryuchkov and A. A. Shalashov (in what
is admittedly a polemic against the Baptist leadership in office
at the time of writing):

> So as to implement persecution on such a scale (as it was
> in the 1930s) and in order to select the more active believers,
> instead of seizing them at random, the agents of the GPU,
> NKVD and later the KGB (secret police) penetrated all
> facets of the Church's organizational life. Thus, under the
> threat of repressions, they enlisted shaky and weak ministers
> of the Church, as well as ordinary believers. The government
> agents wanted answers to the following questions: Where is
> the next church service to be? Who will preach? Who are the
> members of the church council? Which preachers have come
> from outside? Who has made any trips and to what places?
> Who has preached a call to repentance? Who has been pray-
> ing for the imprisoned brethren?
>
> For over thirty years thousands of completely innocent
> Christians have suffered while such activities have con-
> tinued.
>
> During the war (1943–4) the government set up the Coun-
> cil for the Affairs of Religious Cults under the Council of
> Ministers of the U.S.S.R. This body now has supreme
> authority over the Church. At about the same time the All-
> Union Council of Evangelical Christians and Baptists
> (AUCECB) was set up to represent the Church. It was not

elected, but was created by the State authorities. It consisted principally of churchmen who had consented to deviate from evangelical doctrine and agreed to an illegal collaboration with various State authorities. To carry this out, some of them were released from detention before their sentences were completed.

It is quite obvious that after all these massive repressions and because it had been penetrated by numerous government agents of various sorts, the Church was already in fact under illegal State control. Government authorities were moulding the church councils of the local congregations as though they were of clay. They were selecting senior presbyters for the regions and republics from among their own trusted men, and then they were subordinated to the AUCECB.

During the war when churches were re-opened, believers in the main greeted this and the resulting appointment of pastors with such enthusiasm that they did not foresee the deception and danger.

This may seem to us a highly coloured account which sacrifices accuracy to the emotion of the moment. We may be justified in suspecting that it was a less black and white situation than that represented by the writers. Nevertheless, some of the further evidence available to us, scanty though it is, tends to suggest that the writers' accusations were not without some foundation.

For example, we have already pointed out that the 1929 law made specific provision for the direct interference of the State in some Church affairs (particularly in the appointment of the parish executive committees), even though Lenin's pronouncements and the Constitution should have made this impossible. It is not such a large step from this to the wholesale appointment of 'suitable' pastors to important positions, which Kryuchkov and Shalashov say has taken place. Furthermore, evidence of some sort of interference is provided by Mikhail Orlov himself, who stated in 1945 that government officials, men working for the Council for the Affairs of Religious Cults, 'decide the problems of our congregations and take an extremely attentive attitude towards our needs'. Coming from one of the most senior AUCECB officials and published in the *Fraternal Herald*, these words go some way to substantiate what Kryuchkov and Shalashov said. There are other suspicious factors. Although the AUCECB acted under a series of statutes, these were never published, so the guide-lines of its activities remained unknown up to 1960, when they were replaced by a new set. No one, either, has ever seriously claimed that the AUCECB represented any sort of constituency among the believers. Its ten members were certainly not elected by the Church—therefore it is virtually certain that they were appointed by the State. For nearly twenty years (until 1963) they did not even test the strength of their mandate by calling any sort of congress. Finally, there are strong parallels between the AUCECB and the Moscow Patriarchate, which was simultaneously created to preside over the activities of the Russian Orthodox Church.

Despite all these reservations, we can understand the wave of enthusiasm which swept over the Church when the longed-for union of Baptists and Evangelical Christians was achieved, when old heroes of the faith emerged from the dank air of their dungeons or returned from the inhuman conditions of Siberian exile to form a new central administration of the Church in Moscow. It was a time for accepting new mercies with joy and gratitude, not for asking embarrassing political questions or for challenging the integrity of old men who had suffered for their faith. Even now, with the advantage of hindsight, there are not many who would maintain that these men should have remained in their prisons, rather than attempt to grasp the cold, pressured grip of the outstretched hand and attempt to form some sort of working relationship with the man who had extended it.

The first fifteen years of life which the new united Church experienced certainly did not develop in conditions of freedom as western Christians would understand it. For example, it seems that registration of congregations took place only in 1947 and 1948. Many churches which wished to attain this legal status were denied their rights. It was as if the State were granting a freedom of sorts, but at the same time retaining an insurance policy which would enable it to disband congregations at will at any time in the future.

Even so, conditions were infinitely better than during the nightmare which had gone before. Whether compromised or not, Mikhail Orlov, Yakov Zhidkov, Alexander Karev and their associates put life into the new organization, steered it to the end of Stalin's era (1953) without any major disasters and saw it emerge into a life which promised better things with the onset of the 'thaw', the period when Mr. Khrushchev began criticizing the faults of the past. The labour camps began to yield up their victims from 1953 onwards. Many of the most active and uncompromising Baptist pastors and preachers (in much larger numbers than those few who had gained their freedom to head the Union a decade earlier) began to return to their former congregations.

This was an occasion for tension as well as joy. They came like apparitions from another world, for in many instances hope that they were still alive had long since been abandoned. Upon their return they were anxious to resume their work for the spread of the Gospel which had been so long interrupted. They soon discovered that one of the tasks of the All-Union Council was to control the activities of the local congregations and to attempt to keep what they were doing strictly within the limits of the existing legislation. The prisoners who had recently been released had not, of course, been consulted on this compromise—or, if they had, they had remained in prison for declining it.

The All-Union Council contained inherent tensions from the outset. There were doctrinal tensions, as for example when they tried in 1945, with only very limited success, to include Pentecostals within their organization. Neither were the members ever consulted as to which of the doctrinal emphases represented by the Evangelical Christian and Baptist traditions should be encouraged by the new leading body. There was room for some manoeuvre here, but much less so in the strictures (the details of which are unknown) placed by the State on the Church's evangelistic activities and in secular interference in matters such as appointments to religious offices.

As a result of all this, new groupings emerged which were

outside the control of, and partially in opposition to, the All-Union Council. We have only the scantiest information about such movements as the 'Pure Baptists', the 'Free Baptists', the 'Evangelical Christian-Perfectionists', the 'Evangelical Free Christians', the 'Mission of Evangelical Christians' and several other groups. These were active in the 1940s and 1950s and some of them certainly took new inspiration from the return of the prisoners. By the mid-1950s the leadership of some of these groups was in the hands of recent detainees and they found scope for their active work in the uncertain political situation which followed immediately upon the death of Stalin and continued until about 1959. The issues over which they opposed the All-Union Council seem to have been partly doctrinal, but—much more seriously—also political: the nature of the All-Union Council's relations with the State. They also challenged strictures on evangelism. As a Soviet newspaper, the *Baku Worker*, succinctly put it in 1963: "The so-called 'Pure Baptists' demand a more active and diversified religious propaganda and the attracting of a large number of new members into their sect."

Nevertheless, these movements remained regional, diversified and disorganized for several years. The list of their names which we gave above demonstrates this adequately. Looking at the strength of these movements in the Ukraine, we may guess, too, that some who participated in them were motivated less by purely religious ideals than by nationalistic ones. They were not too keen to knuckle down under a leadership which was Moscow-dominated. Yet other groups had sprung up in remote areas of the Soviet Union due to deportation and restriction of movement following release from the camps. Most of these were unregistered and had at best a minimal contact with the central organization. They merely wished to live their Christian lives unmolested.

Then came the catastrophe.

# Chapter IV

# GEORGI VINS THE LEADER

*Khrushchev's Pogrom*

De-Stalinization brought the churches a few years of uneasy peace. Suspect though it seemed to some and undemocratic to most, the All-Union Council of Evangelical Christians and Baptists somehow managed not only to survive but even to show signs of flourishing. Its officials were *persona grata* with the Soviet authorities. Given freedom of action and a continuing relaxation of State pressure, it looked as though it might even be able to begin to represent more faithfully the spiritual interests of the Evangelicals and Baptists, and so draw more and more Protestants under its wing.

But 1960 changed all that. The secret concordat of the war years, observed all this time by both the Baptists and the Russian Orthodox—certainly at least to the extent of taking no initiative to alter the *status quo* all through the years of de-Stalinization—was suddenly broken by the State, which launched a virulent and nation-wide campaign against all forms of religion. The origins of this can be traced to 1957, but it was in 1959–60 that the full force of it descended on the defenceless Church.

The communist offensive at this time was two-pronged. There was a campaign, not stopping short of physical violence, to expropriate congregations from their property and to remove the most active pastors from office. There was also an attempt to use compromised churchmen to undermine Christian defences and morale from within.

Before going into the details of this campaign and its effects on Protestant church life (which will occupy us for the rest of this book), we may stand back and repeat the question which has been so often asked: why was it that, forty years after the

Revolution and with the country apparently set for a period of greater prosperity than it had ever known under Stalin, Khrushchev and his associates found it necessary to launch this crude anti-religious campaign, which was reminiscent of some of the excesses of a bygone era? The orthodox communist answer might be that the country had been pledged ever since the Revolution to eradicate religion as a bourgeois survival, and this was the first time that other preoccupations had not demanded more than their share of attention. Now at last a target date could be set—Khrushchev once mentioned 1980—and the authorities resolved to finish off religion 'at one swoop' (to use a favourite phrase of the anti-religious writers of the time).

It may be doubted whether this is more than a very partial explanation of the new campaign, but it is more likely than another one which has been suggested—that at this time, because of the increasing tension in the Soviet Union's relations with the Chinese, Moscow wanted to demonstrate that its Marxism was 'ideologically pure', despite the de-Stalinization movement which had been begun. Moscow chose to pick on the most defenceless and non-Marxist element in Soviety society, the Church, as a sacrifical victim to Peking's campaign for communist orthodoxy.

The origin of the campaign may, moreover, have been more functional than ideological. Khrushchev was seriously trying to strengthen the recruitment of the Communist Party. He wanted to build up its organization again from the abject state of servility into which it had been forced during the Stalin terror. It is well-known (from the recent Chinese experience, for example) that to keep up the impetus of a revolution there must be enemies at hand to attack. It was not much use whipping up fervent hatred of America and capitalism, because if it were to spill over into excess it would plunge the country on to a collision course and lead to war. In the Soviet Union at that time there were very, very few ideological deviationists—rebel writers, economists with new-fangled theories, bourgeois elements crouched waiting to spring back into capitalism at the crack of a whip—hiding around street corners or plotting in the outhouses of collective farms. There was only one possible enemy represented in every town and village of the land, only one potential victim whose hounding could titillate the nostrils and sharpen the fangs of those who must be trained as ideological warriors, supposedly as successors of the great traditions of 1905 and 1917. This was the Church, or rather the whole religious element in Soviet society, for Muslims, Jews and Buddhists all suffered severely in this new pogrom.

Within the Christian Church, too, the campaign of terror was directed at every group. Here, of course, we shall concentrate entirely upon the Baptists, but there is similar evidence of its impact on the Russian Orthodox Church. Any reader who wishes to read the documents written by Orthodox Christians themselves describing their bitter predicament at this time may do so in the present author's recent book, *Patriarch and Prophets: Persecution of the Russian Orthodox Church Today*.[1] Here one can read of the precise methods used to close some of the ten thousand churches which were expropriated between 1960 and 1964; of the torture and murder of monks in an attempt to intimidate them into vacating all the monasteries of the land; of the trial and imprisonment of some of the leading bishops. As we shall see, the fate which awaited the Baptists was not dissimilar.

The blame for this cataclysmic turn of events must be laid squarely upon the shoulders of the Soviet State and the Communist Party. They took the decision and implemented it, sometimes exploiting the unjust laws to gain their objectives, sometimes simply bypassing them and acting 'administratively' (to use the current Soviet euphemism for 'carrying out a purge').

### New Statutes

There was one further and more subtle aspect of the campaign which has brought bitter internal grief both to the Russian Orthodox Church and to the Baptists during the decade of the 1960s. This was the attempt to exploit the church leadership itself, to intimidate it into an apparent connivance at the purge against religion which was under way.

Both the Orthodox and Baptist administrations, the Moscow Patriarchate and the AUCECB, seem to have taken over a long period something like a Trappist vow of silence on the whole subject of pressure or illegal treatment inflicted on them by the régime. Therefore, despite the undercover tensions which we believe to have existed in both these bodies when the pressure was applied in 1960, they continued to display a face of bland well-being not only to the outside world, but even to their own members inside the Soviet Union (this was despite the fact that Metropolitan Nikolai, a leading figure of the Orthodox Church, was expelled from office at this time—most probably because he made some attempt to resist the new pressures). If this were all, of course, it could easily be explained as an attempt to keep calm in a crisis, and not to respond to provocation in the hope that it would all soon blow over, provided the Church itself did nothing to damage its own cause or exacerbate the situation.

But, unfortunately, there was more to it than this. The Church administration was forced into a situation where it appeared to many Christians as an accessory after the fact—or even worse, to be preparing the Church psychologically for its own demise.

What we have to say here might perhaps be thought to contain considerable elements of doubt. There is one factor, however, which brings our speculations from the realm of possibility into that of virtually proven fact. This is that what happened to the Baptist Church in 1960 was so closely paralleled in the Orthodox Church less than a year later that the only conceivable explanation is this: the train of events, right down to its details, was planned by the anti-religious authorities in Moscow, while the church administrations did their best to make it appear that they were responsible for certain key decisions.

In 1960 the All-Union Council, supposedly on behalf of all Russian Baptists, adopted a set of *New Statutes* to replace those which had been in existence since 1944. These were reinforced by a *Letter of Instructions* which was circulated to all senior presbyters. These two documents in combination appeared to many to attack the very foundations of Christian life. It is our contention that they were not drawn up by the All-Union Council, but simply foisted upon it by the atheist authorities as a major blow in the campaign to destroy religious life. In making this assertion, we are supported not only by a strong body of Russian Baptist opinion, but also by some of the most eminent minds in the Russian Orthodox Church today, who say precisely the same about the amendments made to the Church Regulations by the Holy Synod in 1961 and hastily passed by an uncanonical Synod of Bishops very shortly afterwards.

With the Orthodox Church, power to administer local religious life was taken out of the hands of the parish priest and passed to the three-man executive committee, which, as we already know from the 1929 law, was under the direct control of the communist authorities. This swiftly led, in many instances, to a 'voluntary' vote by a parish for its own closure.

With the Baptists, the situation was more complex. The full text of the *Letter of Instructions* has never been published to this day. Through quotations from it in various secondary sources, however, we know the principal strictures on organized religious life which it contained. The most serious of these concerned young people and their place in church life. Children were to be excluded from services (a provision which is nowhere made in the 1929 law). Furthermore, baptisms (acceptance into full church membership) of mature young people between the ages of eighteen and thirty must be reduced to a minimum. There was also a severe discouragement of evangelistic preaching and a clear injunction to the senior presbyter to restrain 'unhealthy missionary tendencies'.

It is clear that the substance of these instructions amounted to nothing less than a straight denial of many of the ideals which had motivated the ministry of such men as Pavlov, Prokhanov and Odintsov. Was it for this that they had struggled through prison and exile, keeping hold of an uncompromised faith often in completely inhuman conditions? This was the question that many immediately asked themselves.

The more educated among them looked further. They began to analyse the complexities of the *New Statutes* of 1960. We shall not do this here, though the reader who wishes to read more for himself is referred to the full text which is printed in Appendix I of the present author's *Religious Ferment in Russia*[2] and to the analysis of it in Chapter 2 of that book.

These *New Statutes* were almost exclusively concerned with 'control' over church life—hardly at all with the provision of spiritual guidance or with any inspiration to personal holiness. They were much more negative than the Ten Commandments, because they were designed to satisfy the laws of an atheist land, not the moral code of a righteous God. AUCECB regulations, not the Word of God as expressed in the Bible, were to be the ultimate authority for church order. The power of the All-Union Council was taken for granted in these *New Statutes*—but nowhere was it stated whence its authority came. There was no admission that the atheist authorities had any actual control over the Council, yet it was treated as sacrosanct, created for all time by nobody knew whom, self-perpetuating and with no provision for adapting itself to represent the common Baptist mind.

Senior presbyters were to be the main line of communication between the All-Union Council and the local congregations—but it was to be a one-way communication. The latter were given little opportunity to practise the priesthood of all believers. They would find severe restrictions placed on where and when their services were to be held, who should preach to them and even say the prayers. The choir would be allowed to perform only in its own church; all instruments except the organ and the harmonium (and in exceptional cases an upright piano) would be banned from worship. Worst of all, only those congregations which had been fortunate enough to gain registration from the civil authorities might be recognized by the All-Union Council. This was tantamount to saying that the authoritative Baptist body endorsed the ruthless discrimination, and often the naked illegality, of the State's action over registration. Even the registered congregations could not be said to be truly represented by their leadership, but the unregistered ones were to be consigned to a sort of oblivion where they could fall defenceless victims to the persecutions of the local communist authorities.

Such was the formal situation of the Baptist Church when these new internal regulations were promulgated in 1960. The State had dealt a crippling blow to the Church by making it seem as if it were signing its own death warrant. When the unregistered congregations started to fall prey to the atheist campaigners, then the stage was immediately set for dramatic internal developments in Church life.

## The Church's Line of Defence

These developments had three main effects on the Russian Baptists after 1960.

Firstly, the disparate groups, such as the Free Baptists and the Evangelical Christian-Perfectionists, which had in various ways been dissatisfied with the situation of the Protestant Church in the Soviet Union, coalesced into a united movement. Secondly, this new grouping strongly opposed the State's anti-religious policy, attempting to claim their legal and civil rights in an unprecedented way. Thirdly, the would-be reformers opposed the official Baptist leadership (the All-Union Council) and went into schism.

It is not easy, even now, to suggest the probable consequences of this movement for the future of Christianity in the Soviet Union. It may further prove to have an effect on society as a whole, for there were several unexpected features which could have ramifications beyond the specifically Christian sphere.

The most significant feature in this movement was its organization. Bearing in mind the State's fanatical and savage opposition to it from the very first, we hardly exaggerate if we say that there was an element of genius about its organization. The whole situation has about it something of the ring of the persecuted Church of the earliest Christian times, when 'the blood of the martyrs was the seed of the Church', when Christianity triumphed and spread against all human odds.

We are still almost totally without evidence about internal opposition to the All-Union Council before 1960. We know, of course, that the promulgation of the *New Statutes* and *Letter of Instructions* then acted as a direct catalyst in bringing the opposition groups to a united front, but we know nothing of the discussions which led up to this point, and very little of the relations between such bodies as the Free Baptists and the Action Group (*Initsiativniki*)—the latter was the earliest name for the new movement.

The leading brains behind the Action Group seem to have been Alexei Prokofiev, Gennadi Kryuchkov and Georgi Vins. In this book Vins has special mention, not because we believe that he was the most important of the three, but because we happen to know most about him.

The three of them in 1960 seem to have reasoned in something like these terms—if we may take the liberty of summarizing their thoughts: the State, under a period of apparent liberalization, has begun to move back to an almost Stalinist policy—at least so far as the Churches are concerned. It has shown its cynicism by interfering directly in church affairs, both over appointments, and now, with these new regulations, in the total re-orientation of church life to a position where evangelization is eliminated. Worse still, the old leadership has not lifted a finger to protect anyone except itself. They have refused to associate with the very large number of unregistered congregations, which in many areas comprise the chief strength of the Protestant Church. Therefore they have let the State decide those congregations from which they should cut off fellowship. Worse still, the local communist authorities blatantly break the law and disband congregations in many areas. Often those affected appeal to their leaders, but the All-Union Council does nothing at all to intercede for them. We demand a new and stronger leadership. We, as an Action Group, can get this only by holding a Baptist congress, comprised of properly elected representatives from all our congregations in the Soviet Union, both registered and unregistered.

## Brest Baptists

It may sound as if we have put the situation in rather dramatic black and white terms. Yet the earliest documents which we have from the Action Group sometimes put it even more strongly. Passions had been aroused. Prokofiev, Kryuchkov and Vins did not think that the Gospel could be defended by half-measures. We who are not personally involved in the situation may feel that the Action Group put it too strongly when they accused the All-Union Council of connivance at the atheist policy of the régime. Were they in a position to know what representations to the government were being made behind the scenes?

Whatever the answer, the reformers, showing a genius for organization which has characterized much of their activity since, very rapidly made contact with many of the local congregations which were suffering. As the Ukrainian atheist journal, *Man and the World*, put it in November 1966: "The demagogues from the Organizing Committee, the followers of Prokofiev, took it upon themselves to 'protect' these unregistered Baptist groups from the AUCECB and from the 'satanic authorities'."

One particular instance is well known to us. This is how *Soviet Belorussia*, a newspaper published in Minsk, described it (May 12, 1963):

In 1960 the Brest congregation of Evangelical Christians and Baptists united with a similar one at the village of Vulka-Podgorodskaya (Brest District). But only about 100 of the 380 believers would go to Vulka. The rest, incited by their spiritual pastors, Matveyuk, Shepetunko, Kotovich and Fedorchuk, began to organize illegal gatherings in private houses in the town . . . Incited by Matveyuk and his confederates, they pronounced an anathema on the AUCECB and declared themselves to be 'true Christians' and supporters of the so-called 'Organizing Committee'.

This is one of the clearest examples which has ever been printed in the Soviet press of an illegal action being taken against Christians. The 1929 law states unequivocally that only twenty (let alone 380) believers in Brest should have been enough to ensure the formal continuance of Baptist worship in that city. This thriving congregation was obviously expropriated (had there been any justification for this the article surely would have said so) and forced to unite with a much weaker group whose place of worship in a village some distance away was relatively inaccessible. Brest, moreover, is a well-known city, being a frontier town directly on the main railway line connecting Moscow with Warsaw. It is inconceivable that the scandalous action of the authorities in such a prominent place should remain unknown to the All-Union Council in Moscow. Had the Council taken an initiative behind the scenes, this must surely have been intimated to the Brest congregation and the schism there might well have been avoided. As it was, they were almost driven into the arms of the Action Group which was ready to champion their cause. So we know that in this case nearly three-quarters of a one-registered congregation joined the reformers.

It may be that in other instances the All-Union Council did take stronger action. If so, then the Action Group does not seem to have been properly consulted or informed. Had the All-Union Council really been taking any determined stand, however secret, early in the 1960s, it seems unlikely that passions within the Baptist community at this time would have run so high.

The position of the Action Group in its early days is very clear in its broad outlines and there are two generalizations we may make about it. First, the 'action' which it demanded of setting up a congress which would be truly and democratically representative of the whole Baptist movement in the Soviet Union was wholly good and positive. The history of the congresses which have taken place since 1963 amply proves this—they have gone further and further towards meeting these precise demands originally put forward by the Action Group. Second, those who believed in the necessity of an open defence of the Church were prepared to pay for it with their lives, if called upon to do so. Some did. There is no evidence of any such willingness for self-sacrifice on the part of the All-Union Council at this time (though almost all its members had been imprisoned for their faith before the Council was set up).

On the other hand, the All-Union Council has to this day not been able to give to Russian Baptists as a whole any satisfactory or even coherent account of its stewardship from 1959 to 1963. This has not been forgotten. The All-Union Council has never made out any sort of case for the adoption of the 1960 *Letter of Instructions* and the *New Statutes*. The Council did later, admittedly, attempt to back-track and say that they were introduced only on an 'experimental' basis, but the fact remains that they were originally treated as normative and even used by the Soviet courts as a litmus paper for testing loyalty to the régime.

In fact, the regulations of 1960 were an acute embarrassment from the first. After three years the *Letter of Instructions* was cancelled and the *New Statutes* modified—but this was only after the crystallization of serious opposition.

In August 1962, Alexei Prokofiev was arraigned at a rigged trial. His only 'crime' was to have spent the greater part of the previous year in railway trains and aeroplanes, travelling to remote corners of the Soviet Union rallying opinion to support him in his drive for a congress. The support he received was very strong—especially from among the unregistered congregations. It was only to be expected, after all, that if the All-Union Council refused to defend or even associate itself with these groups (as the *New Statutes* said it must not), those who were being discriminated against should support the men who were prepared to come to their defence—Prokofiev, Kryuchkov and Vins.

Prokofiev received a savage sentence of five years in prison, followed by five years in Siberian exile (treading the path which had been worn smooth by so many of his forbears). The reason given for this heavy term of imprisonment was his alleged collaboration with the Germans during the war—an accusation for which no evidence was brought and which was, in any case, totally irrelevant to the case under review.

An insight into the nature of the Soviet campaign against the Action Group in 1962 is provided by an extract from the newspaper *Soviet Moldavia*, which described the demise of Prokofiev. This was printed on January 22, 1963, five months after he had been arrested. We should note that Russian Orthodox bishops, too, were being attacked in similar terms at that time and never was a single one of the accused given any public opportunity to defend himself. We have to conclude, therefore, that the Soviet State was trying to campaign against the Church by whipping up an attitude of popular hysteria against it. No one was given the facts, so not surprisingly some Soviet citizens were inclined to believe the torrent of innuendos, and even blatant lies, which were being heaped upon the heads of innocent and courageous Christians at this time. This is part of what the newspaper said:

Who is this Prokofiev, then? One can't describe the life of

this 'saint' without a feeling of indignation. Under the guise of religious activity, this latter-day 'apostle' shows malice towards everything Soviet, interprets freedom of conscience according to his own whim and breaks our laws. In 1941, at a time of severe trial for our people, he engaged in anti-Soviet propaganda and was convicted as a traitor.

Ten years in prison taught this renegade hypocrite nothing. After his release Prokofiev continued to live like a parasite, organizing illegal Baptist sectarian groups and preaching libellous sermons against the Soviet way of life. He was convicted a second time, but the Soviet State yet found it possible to remit part of his sentence.

'However much you feed a wolf, it will always look towards the forest', says the proverb. Even now punishment failed to deter this dope-peddler. Prokofiev continued to develop his clandestine missionary activity, visiting various towns in the Russian Republic, the Ukraine, Belorussia and Kazakhstan. He penned sermons and letters containing evil aspersions against our system, sending them to all corners of the country. He called on Soviet citizens to renounce earthly blessings, to 'repent of their sins' and to give up work for prayer. 'Every human friendship is no more than debauchery', blathered this obscurantist.

This man has had an especially pernicious influence on young people. He has been trying to kill their inclination towards earthly joys, to disseminate pessimism and scepticism among them. He challenged them to refuse to do military service and to renounce going to the cinema, to theatres and clubs. At Kharkov and in the towns of the Donbass, Prokofiev illegally performed the rites of 'water baptism' on young people. At Zhdanov this obscurantist 'washed' a group of boys and girls in icy water, one of whom, Anatoli Shatsky, a young labourer, developed a severe mental illness.

What does one say in the face of such a torrent of invective? We lack the evidence, of course, to refute it point by point, but one thing can be gleaned even from so manifestly hostile and libellous an account as this: Prokofiev's tireless activity and uncompromising bravery. He was in prison from 1941–51.

Some time in the next decade he served another sentence, and we have no reason to believe it was a particularly short one, despite the remission of sentence. Then at the end of 1962 he was sentenced for a total of another ten years. To us in the West, this type of bravery and devotion seems to belong to a more heroic epoch of the Christian Church. It comes as something of a shock, perhaps, to be confronted with the facts: the age of Christian martyrdom is still very much with us.

The Soviet State has learnt remarkably little from its forty years of conflict with Christianity. The communists consistently misread events because they had no real understanding of the Church's position and probable reactions.

So it happened yet again. They tried to scotch the Action Group movement by cutting off its head. The only visible result of this was that the Action Group gained a martyr and with him an increased determination to press its cause. We can also imagine the embarrassment and moral shame which the All-Union Council must have felt when they saw the State's brutal action in removing their chief rival from the scene just after he had made his initial demand of them.

But the greatest shame of all rests, of course, on the shoulders of the Soviet Government which, forty years after the Revolution, was still incapable of meeting a rival ideology with anything more imaginative or civilized than the creaking apparatus of naked force.

## Georgi Vins

With the removal of Prokofiev, Georgi Vins and Gennadi Kryuchkov took on new responsibilities. It is of some significance that among all the welter of documents which have come to us from the Action Group—or the Reform Baptists, as we shall call them from now on—there is not one which sets out to give us any personal, background details of the leaders of the movement. We can read their devotional literature, follow their political and ecclesiastical struggles, and later read of their bravery in the courts of law and of their sufferings in prison. But of their character, their family background or their education, we are told almost nothing. So, for the present, we can only say that the men are the movement. We can see them only through it. The best testimony to their character is the almost superhuman devotion which the leaders inspired among their followers. Before the demonstration at the Central Committee building in 1966, which we described in the opening chapter, we can hardly discern the personal role played by any individual in the movement.

From verbal reports of some *emigrés* from eastern Europe who used to be active in the Baptist movement on Russian soil in earlier times, we are able to piece together a few details of Vins's background. His father, Peter, of German origin, came from Samara (now Kuibyshev) and was a respected Baptist figure, but he never saw the fruit of his labours. As a young man he was so outstanding that he was encouraged to go to the United States of America to obtain that theological education which was not available to him in Russia, and he went to the Weston Memorial Baptist Church, Philadelphia, just after the Revolution.

From there Peter Vins went to Rochester, New York, to study theology, but a search of the records at the Colgate Rochester Divinity School has failed to provide any information about him. Thence he went on to complete his studies at the Southern Baptist Seminary at Louisville, Kentucky. The records there show that he was in residence from 1919–22. Although he left for home suddenly in March or April 1922, before being ordained, he did receive a degree from Rochester. Immediately upon his return to the Soviet Union, he threw himself into the movement for expansion which was then in full swing, and went off to Siberia as a missionary. He married, and a son was born to him in 1924 in Siberia. This was Georgi and of course he inherited the patronymic 'Petrovich'.

The young child was destined to grow up without his father, unable to benefit from his formative influence or from the Christian wisdom which he had acquired. Peter Vins was one of the earliest victims of the new wave of purges which engulfed the Russian Baptists when Stalinism was established. He disappeared into the prison camps in 1927. Thereafter, the only certain news of him which filtered through was of his death, which occurred in 1929. His suffering was much briefer than that of some others, such as Vasili Odintsov. Boris Pasternak closed his great portrait of Lara, the heroine of *Dr. Zhivago*, with the words, 'One day she went out and did not come back. She must have been arrested in the street, as so often happened in those days, and she died or vanished somewhere, forgotten as a nameless number on a list which was later mislaid.' So it was with Peter Vins.

Peter Vins's influence over his son survived his earthly life. So often in Russian history the political stupidities and brutalities of one generation are visited upon the heads of the next. Was not Lenin profoundly influenced by the execution of his elder brother? Vins's mother, Lidia, must have kept the influence of her husband, with whom she had lived for such a short time, alive before her son's eyes. Indeed she had been and is a remarkable woman, for she took her son to the Ukraine and managed to secure a first-class education for him, despite the fact that he was the son of a man who had died for a 'political offence'. This must have been incredibly difficult. The Soviet régime has consistently discriminated against the children of those who have been purged, even in those many cases where the innocence of the parent was well-known. The Christian son of a religious family would have found the going even more difficult. Lidia Vins still stands by her son's side.

Georgi Vins graduated about the time of the end of the Second World War. He is reputed to have gained no less than two degrees, one in economics and the other in engineering. He took a job in Kiev as an economist and was not engaged in full-time work as a Baptist pastor for some years.

It was Khrushchev's new anti-religious policy, apparently, which challenged him to change the whole direction of his life. It is said (although there is no documented evidence of this) that A. L. Andreyev, the senior Baptist pastor in Kiev, was among the handful of notorious religious collaborators with the communist régime. We will not press the point, for he is now dead and unable to defend himself. The story goes that as soon as the first icy draughts of the new policy were felt, Andreyev went much further than was necessary to justify it publicly before his congregation. Vins challenged him. There was a sharp personal clash between the two men. Andreyev reacted with a personal bitterness towards Vins which was totally out of keeping with his standing as a Christian minister, and virtually threw the younger man into the arms of the Reform Baptists. It is very important to note that Vins was loyal to the All-Union Council up to this time. He was not associated with the Free Baptists or any of the earlier opposition groups.

This incident seems to have constituted Georgi Vins's 'calling' as a pastor, for from this time onwards he was probably engaged full-time in Christian administrative and pastoral work. On the administrative side, we shall have plenty of opportunity to review the progress of the movement which he and Kryuchkov were soon to lead. We should not, however, overlook his greatness as a pastor. He and his fellows had had no formal theological education, yet one of the outstanding features of the Reform Baptist movement, which we encounter again and again, is its consistent and intense concern for the spiritual and physical well-being of its members.

Georgi Vins and six other leaders of the Reform Movement addressed all young Baptist parents in 1964. They provide a practical manual of guidance on how to bring up children as Christians amidst the massive atheism of the system. This document has been virulently attacked in the press as anti-Soviet. It certainly does not instruct young parents to bring up their children as communists! Yet to attempt to turn it into a political declaration is farcical. Of its quality, the reader must judge for himself from this extract, probably the most sensitive passage (from the authorities' point of view) which it contains:

> Dear brother and sister! ... If your children are with you, do they know the Lord? Do they love people? Are they constant in the Lord's teaching and precepts, as He commanded? (Eph. 6:4) The Word of the Lord challenges believing parents to instruct their children about Him ...
>
> The greatest possession which you must acquire and pass on to your children is the priceless one of faith ... By your children it may be judged how you yourself value the gift of faith and what the Lord means to you!
>
> Dear parents! Will not your own children, standing with-

out, bear witness against you with tears on that day? Is your salvation secure?

If all in your family are believers, then can they all be called your household church and can Christ be called their glory? ...

Beloved brother and sister, if you know any brothers or sisters who do not come to worship, and who have perhaps abandoned their Lord, then take care of them for the sake of their salvation.

Georgi Vins and the other leaders of the Reform Movement have taken a strong stand on a number of issues. Let us not forget that one of them is a direct and uncompromising application of rigid Christian principles to life in a communist State.

## Aida Skripnikova

In talking of the Baptist congregation at Brest, we have already hinted at the quality of support the leaders of the Reform Movement were able to command. Very much of it came from young people. In many areas, a Soviet atheist article tells us, the words 'Reform Baptists' (*Initsiativniki*) rapidly became synonymous with 'young Baptists'. A constant thread uniting the propaganda articles denouncing them in the Soviet press is that young people have been activated by this new presentation of a practical Gospel (though this is not the phraseology the atheists use, of course). We shall later have the opportunity of looking at the ages of those Baptists who have been imprisoned in recent years. The proportion of young people among them is staggering.

One of those young people was Aida Skripnikova, a girl who was only eighteen years old when the Reform Movement began. She first came into prominence later that year when, on New Year's Eve 1961, she distributed cards on which she had typed out one of her own religious poems appropriate to the occasion. For this she was bitterly attacked in *Smena*, a young people's newspaper, in an article entitled, 'Don't be a corpse among the living'. When this happened, she immediately started to consider a reply. When she had written it, she circulated the text in

Leningrad. Those who were given it had received into their hands some of the most remarkable pages ever to have been written by a young Russian Christian. They are worth quoting at some length (the full text runs to nearly four thousand words and can be found in *The Religious Situation*, *1969*, Beacon Press, Boston, Mass., pp. 74–84) because they show the spiritual calibre of the type of person who was attracted into Vins's movement.

Let us talk àbout your article, Valen Ivanovich.[3] Let us imagine that you and I have decided to compete against each other in a race. And suddenly you tie my legs together and rush towards the finishing post. "Hurray! I've won!" you cry triumphantly. "Untie my legs! Set me free! Then we'll see who'll win," I say. "Untie your legs? Set you free? But this would be an encroachment upon my freedom!" you answer . . .

If *you* suddenly feel like spending some time amongst your close friends you do not have to be afraid that by doing this you will break the law. *You* can meet together at any time and do whatever you like—talk, read or sing. Why, then, can *we* not visit one another? What law forbids this? Why can we not pray, or read the Bible whenever we want? We are allowed to speak about God only in church. You would certainly not accept it if you were allowed to talk about the theatre only in a theatre or about books only in a library. In the same way, we cannot be silent about what constitutes the whole meaning of our life—about Christ.

Wherever it is we meet, whether in church or in a private apartment, we talk about Christ everywhere. You call our small friendly meetings illegal, but Christ sanctioned the right to meet; he said, "Where two or three are gathered together in my name, there am I in the midst."

"No one forbids you to believe in God," you say. We believe, not because you generously give us permission. We would go on believing even if you were to forbid it. We are Christians not because 'religious liberty' is inscribed in the constitution of the U.S.S.R., but because Christ died on Golgotha . . .

And then you do not like us distributing religious letters. Imagine that a fire has started and that you must warn people of the danger, wake them up. You would sound the alarm, but if there should be no alarm bell near at hand, you would grab hold of any old bucket, even one full of holes, and would begin filling it. No one would blame you for using an old, useless bucket in those circumstances.

Allow us to publish a mass-circulation newspaper which can be bought at a kiosk—and I assure you we would not need to distribute religious letters.

If you do not like our holding prayer meetings in private apartments, then allow us to study the Bible in church, allow us to hold small meetings of young people in church, allow us to meet in *our* church whenever we want.

You are mistaken when you say that we have 'recently been seized by an insatiable desire for prayer meetings organized in private apartments'. It is incorrect to say 'recently'.

When I was very small, people very often met in our apartment to read the Bible and to pray. They met, despite the cruel persecution that could result (1947). They went on meeting even after the night when several people were arrested. After spending between eight and ten years in prison, these people again began meeting to read the Bible and to pray. We also meet and you can do nothing about it . . .

It is absurd to announce that, if believers were to be given freedom, this would be 'an infringement of the workers' freedom of conscience'. How could it constitute such an infringement if a Christian periodical, such as *The Young Christian* or *Joyful News*, were to lie beside *Komsomol Truth* in a kiosk? Only those who wished to would buy our periodicals. People could read the article, "Don't be a corpse among the living!" in *Smena* and they would be able to read a reply to it in *The Young Christian*. This is no more than justice—and only in this way can one interpret freedom.

You write: "We atheists are not against eternal life, but it must exist here on earth, not in a world beyond. Immortality consists for us not, as religion promises, in sitting idly in some sort of Elysian field, munching sticky buns and unconcernedly watching the larger part of humanity suffer agony in fiery Gehenna."

I do not know what 'religion promises', but the Word of God says this: "For the Kingdom of God is not meat and drink; but righteousness, and peace, and joy in the Holy Spirit" (Rom. 14:17).

You write: "Man achieves immortality through his work."

Even the very fact that you talk about immortality shows that, despite your atheism, you find it hard to conceive that you will disappear for ever. From your point of view, we can do no more than talk, firstly, about the immortality of great men such as Pushkin,[4] Lomonosov,[5] Beethoven and, if you wish, Gagarin; and secondly about that of men who create material things . . .

In your opinion, "there is no nobler, brighter or more beautiful goal in the world than that of building communism and living under it". And you ask me whether I am prepared to work for this goal.

No, I do not want to work for this goal, because I consider it neither bright nor noble. The society which you will build will never be just, because you yourselves are unjust. I am deeply convinced that where there is no truth, there can be no happiness either! The goal of my life is to serve the truth.

My father refused to kill people. You call this a crime. He refused to kill people and for this he lost his own life. He died in order not to kill. If everyone were prepared to die rather than to kill, then there would be no wars. Christ said, "Do not kill." You jeer at this commandment. If only people would remember it! But today some have forgotten it, others jeer at it and that is the only reason why the threat of war now hangs over the world . . .

"Your father," you say, "refused to take up arms to defend you." You say 'defend'. I know Baptists who did take up arms to defend their children, their homeland. But today in this country, in the country which they defended, they are rejected; they are not trusted, they are forbidden to meet freely for prayer, a whole stream of crude lies pours down upon them and they are told, "There is no room for you in our beautiful world!"—"You're getting in our way!"—"We'll isolate you!"—"We'll punish you!" . . .

You write: "Innumerable are the crimes of all religions, including the Baptist faith, before humanity and particularly before science . . ."

Jan Hus[6] was burnt by men who called themselves Christians. He said: "Oh, Lord Jesus Christ, I am ready to bear with joy a cruel and terrible death for the sake of your shining Gospel and for preaching your Holy Word. Forgive, I beseech Thee, all my enemies . . . For the main goal of all my preaching, teaching, writing and other works was to save men from sin. And now I am called before the Roman Curia to answer for preaching the Gospel."

Today you do not want to admit that Jan Hus was burnt as a preacher of the Gospel. And this is quite understandable. You, after all, are also persecuting men for preaching the Gospel. And if you were to admit that Jan Hus was executed for preaching the Gospel, you would by this very admission condemn yourselves.

If Jan Hus had lived in our time, in our country, he would have been thrown into prison . . .

Here is the last point to which I would like to draw your attention. You are shocked that God destroyed all men, except Noah's family. The ark was built in 120 years; for this length of time men heard the words, "Come in!"—"Receive salvation"—"Repent". At last, the ark was ready—and even then its doors remained open for six days. Anyone who wished could go in. But people did not want to. They perished—and it was simply because they did not wish to be saved. You have many times already heard God's call: "Repent before it is too late! Repent and inherit eternal life! Come to Christ!"

Just as in the past men were offered the ark as a means of salvation, so have we been given Christ. But you do not wish to receive him, you do not wish to receive eternal life. God offers you this life, but you do not wish to receive it. God offers you this life but you reject the opportunity. Whom will you blame on the Day of Judgment? Who will bear the guilt for your downfall? Will it not be you yourselves? You were offered salvation so many times, but you did not want to 'enter the ark'.

But today you can still change your fate. Before it is too late,

COME TO CHRIST.


Aida Skripnikova writes as a person of intelligence and vivacity. From her photograph, she is also extremely beautiful. But without any doubt her greatest quality is her faith and her uncompromising bravery in proclaiming it. These words come from a girl of eighteen—thrown into the jaws of a system which had already devoured her father! The challenge which she issued was precisely such as the All-Union Council most feared. They have consistently maintained the attitude that such action endangers the well-being of the majority of Baptists in the Soviet Union. Whether they believe these words in their innermost being—and whether they are right in what they say—each one of us must judge for himself.

Aida was arrested shortly after she had distributed her reply to the article in *Smena*. Her imprisonment lasted for a year and we do not know what she suffered. Who is to say that this young girl of eighteen was any less brave than Jan Hus? Such are the victims of present-day Soviet religious persecution.

It was, not surprisingly, the Reform Baptists under Vins and Kryuchkov who came to the defence of this remarkable girl and sent out of the country information about her imprisonment. Like the early Christians, she was not crushed by her experience. After her release in 1964, she was attacked by several newspapers, including *Izvestia*. Four years of continual harassment (conditional liberty, interspersed with interrogations and short spells in prison)—and then Aida, twenty-four and mature in Christian suffering, was arrested once again in Leningrad, after a pile of Christian literature and personal possessions had been removed from her apartment. In July 1968 she was sentenced to three years and at the time of writing she is in the Potma prison complex. But one seriously asks the question: how many Aida Skripnikovas does it take to leaven the whole lump of the younger generation in Russia today?

*The 1963 Congress*

The Reform Baptist movement led by Prokofiev (before his arrest) and by Kryuchkov and Vins made the demand for an All-Union Baptist congress the cardinal point in its programme. In formulating this it rapidly demonstrated how widespread was the dissatisfaction with the Moscow leadership of the Russian Baptist Church, especially among the unregistered congregations whom the latter refused to represent. This lack of confidence was put most succinctly by the group of Baptists from Kiev under Vins's leadership. This is how they summed up the situation:

> The religious centre called the All-Union Council of Evangelical Christians and Baptists, which is now in existence, has not been elected by the local Evangelical Christian and Baptist churches, has not been authorized by them and does not represent them. The members of the All-Union Council have long since cut themselves off from the believing masses, followed the path of dictatorship and abolished the rights of local churches to self-determination . . . The Organizing Committee [a later name for the Action Group], together with the whole Church, censures the All-Union Council . . . for including in the Union only one-third of the communities (the registered ones), while two-thirds (the unregistered ones) have not been recognized by it.

Even before the arrest of Prokofiev, the reformers had formulated a precisely-drafted revision of the 1960 *New Statutes* which they wished to see come up for discussion at a future congress. The key point in this new draft was that the All-Union Council should be elected by a congress. These elected representatives should meet in plenary session to carry out the main business of the Church at least once every six months. The reformers also wished to see senior presbyters elected from below, not appointed from above, and they demanded that the local congregation should have more freedom to govern its own affairs without continual outside interference, either from the autocratic action of senior presbyters or the much less acceptable manipulations of the local communist authorities.

The summary dismissal of these demands by the All-Union Council without any adequate discussion (at least with none which has gone on record) led to a rapid exacerbation of the situation. No satisfactory channels of communication were set up between the reformers and the All-Union Council. To make things very much worse, a wave of arrests began in 1961–2 (even before Prokofiev himself was removed) in which many of the most active reformers were removed to places where they were unlikely to be able to hold conversations with anyone, except perhaps a criminal in the next cell.

To the Reform Baptists, this turn of events—with the State stepping in to remove some of the best members of their move-ment—must have seemed like a very unholy alliance between the official Church and the State. Only in this light can we understand their drastic action in assuming powers of leader-ship in lieu of elections by a free and representative congress, which they judged would never be held. At his trial in 1966, Kryuchkov gave convincing evidence[7] that they had taken this step only after being urged to do so by masses of people from the local congregations who pledged their support in thousands. Even the prosecutor admitted that 'they have been elected and enjoy wide support among Baptists'.

One of the first acts of these new leaders who had come for-ward was to do something which still rankles bitterly today. In June 1962, they excommunicated Yakov Zhidkov, Alexander Karev and most of the other top leaders of the All-Union Council, as well as those senior presbyters whom they con-sidered to have yielded under pressure.

We are, of course, still lacking much of the essential evidence upon which this decision was based, particularly as regards the individual personalities of the All-Union Council. It has seemed to many people the one action which gave the All-Union Council a legitimate cause of grievance and which risked discrediting the work the reformers were trying to do. While so much evidence is lacking, it would be wrong for us to come to firm conclusions about this particular action. The reformers *could* not have known the personal circumstances of all the twenty-seven men whom they excommunicated. How did they know whether or not these men had made secret representations to the Soviet Government to get the situation changed for the better? Was it the will of the majority of Baptists that these excommunications—after all, the gravest sentence, since the burnings of the Middle Ages, which one Christian can pass on another—should take place? These are serious questions which we cannot answer. This step has been defended as democratic by one of the reformers in a lengthy justification,[8] but it is naturally still a source of bitterness hindering the attempts to achieve a Baptist re-unification.

There is not the slightest doubt, furthermore, that the reform leaders acted under severe provocation. The 1960 *New Statutes* and *Letter of Instructions* seemed a direct betrayal of the Church at that time. They still seem so in retrospect, even though they have been abolished. The All-Union Council, of course, has never been able, in any of its public statements, even to begin to justify itself for what it did. Indeed how *could* it say (assuming this to be true), "We adopted these regulations under terrorist threats from the secret police"?

The Editor of the *Baptist Times* (London), the Rev. Walter Bottoms, has enquired about this matter in Moscow and sees the 1960 situation in a different light. He puts it thus (in a private communication to the author):

My own personal interpretation, which has never been denied by any to whom I have spoken, is that the Union officers accepted the *New Statutes* under some such threat [as closure of all church buildings], hoping that by accepting on paper they could in practice get round them. This has been a familiar tactic by Baptists in Spain. Unfortunately in Russia some of the senior presbyters (district superintendents) applied the *New Statutes* with severity and vigour. The result was that many churches and ministers revolted and so the anti-Union movement began. When this grew, the officers of the Union were able to say in effect to the Minister of Religious Affairs: 'Now see what you have done! If you do not allow us to call off these statutes you will have a full-scale revolt on your hands!' What is certain, on the evidence of the brethren in Moscow, is that the *New*

*Statutes* were accepted only after strenuous representations by the officers of the Union.

Whatever really happened in Moscow when these changes took place, we know that there were personal incidents involving reformers which were much more directly provocative. For example, it happened on several occasions that when zealous reformers were brought to court by the Soviet authorities, senior presbyters were called to give testimony against them—and complied. A member of a registered congregation writes of this period:

> Many were convicted. Our dear brethren raised a cry and it reached us, members of the registered congregations. Anyone who heard this cry and made an attempt to give them the necessary help was driven out of the church. This exclusion meant that he would be considered not as someone who had suffered for the evangelical faith, but as someone who had 'broken the law.'

Any observer impartially surveying the scene must feel extreme disquiet at this alleged connivance by a Christian body in the policy of an atheist authority. For as long as the All-Union Council allowed such a situation to continue, they were likely to widen the gulf between themselves and the Reform Baptists. The above quotation, making them appear as willing accomplices, does in fact come to us from a compilation of Vins's supporters (the *Messenger of Salvation*), but there are no grounds whatsoever to doubt that they culled it from a *bonafide* member of a registered congregation. All the evidence suggests most strongly that when the *New Statutes* were introduced in 1960, the Baptist authorities consistently urged that they must be kept. Discussion on whether the new regulations compromised the essentials of the evangelical faith was entirely discouraged. Indeed, as early as 1961, before there had been any adequate time for discussion, Alexander Karev, the General Secretary of the All-Union Council, stated, when speaking to young people in the Moscow Baptist Church:

> The *Statutes* and the *Letter of Instructions* are the es-

sence, the two rails along which our brotherhood is moving.
They are founded upon the law. To refuse to recognize these
documents is to refuse to recognize the law; this in turn
entails refusal to recognize the Soviet State, which is the
same as to oppose it.

From the State's point of view, the situation was quite un-
ambiguous—"Join the congregations under the All-Union
Council, or else . . .!" In other words, for a Baptist to refuse to
accept the *New Statutes*, which were technically an internal
church matter, was interpreted by the State as an illegal act,
meriting up to three years' imprisonment. *Soviet Justice*, one of
Russia's most authoritative legal periodicals, declared (No. 9,
1964) of a Baptist community in Western Siberia:

> In Kulunda an unregistered congregation of Evangelical
> Christians and Baptists had existed for a long time. They
> preached the Bible and observed the religious practices laid
> down by the All-Union Council. From 1961 all kinds of
> addresses, notices and other texts criticizing the All-Union
> Council began to appear amongst the Baptists. From this
> time the activities of some of the community's members as-
> sumed a reactionary character.
> In November 1962 the chairman of the Kulunda Settle-
> ment Council demanded that the community either be
> registered or cease holding meetings.
> The older members obeyed, but the younger ones, with
> Subbotin at their head, broke away. They began holding
> illegal meetings at night. This section of the Baptists refused
> to recognize the official All-Union Council statutes and
> evaded the control of the laws on religious cults in force in
> the Soviet Union.

In other words, as members of this very congregation put it
in a document written just before this article appeared in
*Soviet Justice*, a congregation which criticized the constitution
of the All-Union Council was *de facto* barred from registration
and its members had committed an offence indictable under
article 142 or 227 of the Penal Code. This raises unprecedented

legal questions which we cannot discuss here. The All-Union Council annulled the *Letter of Instructions* and modified the statutes in 1963 (indeed, *before* the article we have quoted was written). Nevertheless, it seems that failure to comply with the revised version of the statutes was interpreted by the State as an even more serious offence. Such seems to have been the case with the Kulunda Baptists, especially with the martyr, Nikolai Khmara, whose story we shall be telling later in this chapter.

The emendation of the *New Statutes* occurred at a Baptist congress hastily convened in October 1963. It was very remarkable that there should have been a congress at all, let alone at this particular time. There had been none since the formation of the All-Union Council twenty years before. 1960 to 1964 were the blackest years for all religious denominations since the purges of the 1930s. So the fact that the State allowed a congress to be convened during this very period of persecution shows that it was severely worried by the pressure which was being applied by Georgi Vins and his fellow-reformers.

The 1963 congress was unrepresentative of the Russian Baptist movement as a whole. The leaders of the All-Union Council made a fundamental error. They failed to consult adequately with Georgi Vins and his associates in the setting up of the conference. Many congregations had by this time been illegally deprived of their registration by the State, but there was no attempt to ensure that they were represented. To be unregistered was simply to be an outcast. Not only were Vins and Kryuchkov deprived of even a token representation on the platform; they later claimed that they had not even been informed that the congress would be taking place. Furthermore, at least a hundred and fifty of the movement's most active supporters were by this time held in prison. No wonder that Vins later dubbed it a 'pseudo-congress'! How could it, in the circumstances, have achieved anything at all? (Moscow Baptist officials have stated verbally, we should add, that the reformers were invited to attend, but refused to do so unless Karev and all the other officers of the All-Union Council resigned before the congress opened.)

It comes as a surprise, then, to find that some genuine concessions were in fact made to the demands of the reformers. They were mostly minor ones, but they do very clearly demonstrate that the All-Union Council wished to initiate a reconciliation. Among their number, there must have been some people who advocated very strongly that this should take place. At the end of the congress it circulated a message to all congregations (including unregistered ones) in which a note of genuine anguish at their disunity can be discerned. The Council also made the bold promise that in future it would defend the rights and interests of individual churches and ministers before the State authorities. However, the events which immediately followed gave little indication that they intended to stand by these brave words.

Perhaps the most important concession to the demands of the reformers was that the principle was established of regular congresses in the future, to be held at three-yearly intervals. Not only that, but the All-Union Council, which seems to have been appointed by the State at its foundation, was to be elected by the congress from now on. Unfortunately, however, the mechanics of this particular congress ensured a communist-style election, in which no genuine alternative candidates appeared and which seemed to be designed to preserve the *status quo*. Georgi Vins cannot have been reassured to see all the same old faces firmly back in office, with none of his own supporters given a vote.

Despite the demands of the reformers, senior presbyters (district superintendents) continued to be appointed by the All-Union Council, not elected from below, but there was a positive gain in local church life: from now on anyone, not only recognized ministers, would be allowed to preach.

The very serious stumbling-block, the *Letter of Instructions*, was revoked, so the reformers were no longer able to say that the All-Union Council was propagating a series of anti-evangelical principles. Nevertheless, the reformers could still complain that the constitution now adopted made no mention of what had been set out as the fundamental task of the Evangelical Christians and the Baptists in their original separate constitutions: the spreading of the Gospel.

Vins, in rejecting the competence of the October 1963 con-

gress to take any decisions on behalf of the Baptist movement
in the Soviet Union, was nevertheless extremely positive in his
resulting action. Firstly, he replied in depth and in a conciliatory tone to continuing accusations against him by the All-
Union Council. Secondly, he increased his pastoral concern for
those he was supporting. Thirdly, he had a hand in organizing
one of the most remarkable initiatives in recent Soviet history,
when he helped set up the Council of Baptist Prisoners' Relatives. Let us look at each of these activities in turn.

## Vins and the All-Union Council

Vins was not content to state his continuing disagreement with
the All-Union Council and to leave it at that.

He immediately set himself the task of composing a detailed
theological justification for his position. This was discussed by
the reformers in July 1964, and by October 21 Vins and his
associates had written this up into forty-one closely-packed
pages of intense and intricate theological reasoning. It was entitled *Address to all Servants of the Evangelical Christian and
Baptist Church, to all Brothers and Sisters who Comprise the
Church of Our Lord Jesus Christ*, and six brothers besides Vins
signed it. It is to be presumed that those who refer to the
leaders of the Reform Movement as upstarts, or who interpret
their action as being simply a bid to grab the leadership, have
never read this document.

It is a treatise of applied theological reasoning on the theme
of sanctification, based on the scriptural texts, 'For this is the
will of God, even your sanctification' (1 Thess. 4:3) and
'Follow peace with all men, and holiness, without which no man
shall see the Lord' (Heb. 12:14). The authors set out in general
terms what sanctification means for the Christian today and
how it may be achieved step by step, receiving purification
through repentance and the grace of God. At every point in the
treatise the reasoning is fully substantiated with quotations
from the Scriptures. It is a theology to undergird a programme
of action, as the conclusion makes abundantly clear: "Beloved,
we know and are sure in the Lord that our call to practical acts
of purification and sanctification will be the occasion of joy and

praise among all the true children of God." To read it in full is
a humbling experience.

An anonymous supporter of the Reform Movement
answered in detail the accusations which were being brought
against Vins, Kryuchkov and their programme by the All-
Union Council. He sets out to answer the specific allegations in
turn, but after raising the fifth allegation, the document breaks
off and its continuation has never become available to us. Here
is a summary of what he says:

1. The All-Union Council dislikes the way in which the
Vins–Kryuchkov group has been distributing letters to believers. Yet what other way is there in current conditions of making
one's case known?

2. Why do the reformers try and recruit followers from within
existing congregations under the All-Union Council, instead of
trying to make new converts to follow them? Why not adopt a
new name and leave the brotherhood in peace? These questions
are formulated by people who do not wish to be forced to face
uncomfortable issues.

3. 'They are slandering brethren of long standing.' There is a
difference between slander and speaking the truth, however uncomfortable that truth may be.

4. The All-Union Council has consistently maintained that
the reformers were badly at fault to excommunicate it, especially as they were in no formal ecclesiastical position to do so.
After quoting the New Testament precedents for the act of ex-
communication, the writer states that the very act of promul-
gating the *New Statutes* and the *Letter of Instructions* proved
that the All-Union Council was actively co-operating with the
atheists. Before going to the extreme of pronouncing the ex-
communication, the Action Group had tried all methods of
persuasion which were open to them. The decisions on whom
to excommunicate were made democratically by the local congregations—the only people in possession of the facts upon
which such a judgment could be based. Sometimes the All-
Union Council transferred to other regions pastors whose
guilt had been exposed to protect them in their dubious
activities.

5. Even if the All-Union Council were guilty, did not condemnation of its members cause unnecessary divisions? The All-Union Council consistently refused to have dealings with unregistered congregations. Therefore Prokofiev, Vins and Kryuchkov acted precisely to try and ensure the unity of both registered and unregistered congregations. A free congress alone could have resolved the situation. The writer was himself a member of a registered community, and he knows from his own personal experience that to attempt to help entailed being cut off from the fellowship of the registered congregation.

This writer whose arguments we have been summarizing goes on to explain that it was for the specific purpose of helping these groups who had been artificially isolated from fellowship, of giving them a feeling of solidarity and of forming some sort of organization for their protection, that the reformers set up a new administrative body which was formally quite separate from the All-Union Council.

It seems that it was the way the October 1963 Congress was convened and conducted which finally convinced Kryuchkov and Vins that it was impossible to look for any basic reform or change of attitude in the All-Union Council. On March 23, 1965, the excommunications were confirmed and the leading reformers met secretly in Moscow on September 18–19 to establish their movement under the new name, 'The Council of Churches of the Evangelical Christians and Baptists'. A constitution was adopted. This was the moment at which the schism among the Russian Baptists became official. It still persists. Though the All-Union Council has since made a number of attempts to heal it, these have had only a limited success. This is in no small measure due to the unremitting hostility of the State to the reformers. The All-Union Council could not very well conduct unity negotiations with men who were in prison, after all.

## Vins as Pastor

Apart from his capacity as organizer and pastor, Georgi Vins is a pastor and a poet, a poet moreover, who sometimes puts his verse to unusual purposes. In April 1965 he gave Alexander Karev one of his works and we give some extracts from it below:

### TO A. V. KAREV

No! These Church matters will not die!
No more than Christ's love will die,
Than the living word will die
Which brings us salvation.
No! The matter of the congress will not die! . . .[9]
I loved you as a pastor and champion,
And have listened to your word with delight.
I saw in you an ambassador of the Creator,
A servant of Christ in our difficult times!
And I was not alone in loving you sincerely,
Loving you as a brother, as a dear friend.
But then a fearful year came for the Church—
I did not know you, I saw in you another.
I languished waiting for your appeal . . .
But instead of that you gave another bread,
Saturated with the poison of betrayal.
Then atheism, furthered by your hand,
Pushed us on the road of universal downfall!
You annulled the command of Christ . . .
The Church sorrowed, knowing what awaited you,
For God sees all that is secret; He knows all.
The blood of the martyrs cries out to God,
He counts every orphan tear!
And this path has brought you into shame—
Compromise with atheists is no good way!
No, you are outside the Church,
Outside God's brotherhood of Evangelical Baptists.
Now you speak of love;
You call to union and to common work.
Remember the blood of Christ
And the great work of the Gospel!
But your call sounds somewhat strange,
For it ignores repentance, chief of all! . . .
I understand; it's hard for you to admit

Your fault, for the way has been very long . . .
The glory of earthly days will not save you,
Nor your clever diplomatic mastery,
Nor the melodious cadence of your preaching,
Nor the closeness to God which you once had!
The way of repentance alone you need!
Save your soul while your heart still beats! . . .
I used to love you, but now I only sorrow,
Remembering the way of the heroes of the faith.
I loved the persecuted Russian brotherhood
Which goes forward, making no concessions!
The blood of the sufferers, being shed in battle
For the sacred truth, for Christ,
Will waken many to sincere prayer
And will lead them to the foot of the cross!
I believe that God will lead to victory.
Unity will be pure and holy.
The whole Russian brotherhood will follow the Lord
In love of unity, in joyful tranquillity.
There will be a congress, a gathering of Christ's friends—
There a Latvian brother will embrace a Belorussian brother
In the family of Christ, both free and holy.
Emissaries will come from the Ukraine, Siberia,
Moldavia and severe Vorkuta,
Osetins will come from the Caucasus Mountains
To the joyful festival of dreams now realized . . .
I used to love you, but now I weep!
Oh, make your peace with God, I pray!
And, loving your poor soul,
I summon you to the Heavenly Father.

We have quoted this remarkable poem at length because it
demonstrates the intense concern of Georgi Vins for the soul of
another man. If such a call to repentance seems arrogant to us,
let us remember that it is an arrogance which is shared by
Amos, Isaiah and St. John the Baptist. The cry of 'The Lord is
at hand' has always been a hard one for Christians to hear,
because it implies judgment as well as joy.
This poem also happens to be the only major document

which we have from the hand of Georgi Vins alone. It confirms that he is a man of sensibility and broad vision, as well as uncompromising devotion to a cause.

When Vins and Kryuchkov emerged as leaders of the Reform Movement after the arrest of Prokofiev, they also demonstrated their pastoral concern for their people in a series of important writings and in actions of remarkable courage.

For example, they have written a series of articles teaching families how to remain faithful to the Gospel under conditions of Soviet atheism. These are far more outspoken than anything the All-Union Council has ever been able to publish. As a result Vins and his friends have been denounced and abused by the Soviet authorities; atheist writers dub these the 'accursed' works of the Organizing Committee. We quoted at length from one of these above.[10]

Equally impressive is the *Fraternal Leaflet* of July 1965, where the reformers show intense pastoral concern for everyone who has in any way helped them with their work:

> The people of God are fighting to make discord and disorder in the Church yield to creativity and sanctity ... Today the results of these sacred efforts have become evident to many—results achieved by prayer, fasting, hard work and struggle. The Lord is vouchsafing His rich blessing. The Church is literally being raised up from its bed of sickness and is being healed of its serious ailment ...
>
> We shall pray that this healing may touch every brother and sister, every local church, to the spiritual benefit of the whole people of God and to the glory of God the Father and of our Lord Jesus Christ ...
>
> We sincerely greet you, our brother-ministers of the Churches of Christ, who are caring unceasingly for the children of God committed to your charge by the Lord and are effecting their consecration. "Take heed therefore unto yourselves and to all the flock, over which the Holy Ghost hath made you overseers, to feed the church of God, which He hath purchased with His own blood" (Acts 20:28) ...
>
> We greet you, our brother and sister workers who have been duplicating our fraternal letters and appeals; we praise

the Lord for your hard and self-sacrificing work which is so important at this time . . .

We greet all you who sincerely collaborate by appending your signatures to petitions for permission to hold a congress, all who receive our ministers and provide your houses where the people of God may worship.

## Defence of Prisoners

Nowhere, however, is the intense pastoral concern and the personal bravery of the reform leaders more clearly demonstrated than in their unceasing action on behalf of those who have suffered imprisonment for their faith.

After the Baptist congress of October 1963, the focus of our attention must move from the relations of the All-Union Council and the new schismatic body with each other to the increasing savagery of the State's campaign against anyone who showed the slightest inclination to stand up for his rights.

The State gave permission for the congress to be held presumably because it was embarrassed by the activities of Kryuchkov, Vins and their followers, and feared that they might stir up a great deal of popular support in the incipient human rights movement. Yet instead of allowing a breathing period of relative calm, in which, perhaps, they might have released the prisoners, hoping for a reconciliation in the resulting atmosphere of good will, further arrests followed almost immediately, at the end of 1963 and the beginning of 1964. At Kulunda, in Western Siberia, there occurred one of the most scandalous trials of recent Soviet history. The subsequent murder of an innocent man in prison may have been the work of an individual, sadistic prison administrator, but he was never brought to justice and the case of those convicted was never reviewed. Official Soviet policy had created the conditions in which such dreadful incidents could occur.

The Kulunda Baptists were a dedicated group of people who had consistently been denied registration by the Soviet authorities. They could not therefore legally meet for worship at all, let alone possess a building to pray in. So they were forced to meet in cramped conditions in private apartments (the open air was of course impossible in the bitter Siberian winter). They also had to keep their meetings as secret as possible to avoid summary arrest by the police and the imposition of crippling fines upon them.

Nevertheless, they attracted the attention of people untouched by the Gospel. One of these was Nikolai Kuzmich Khmara. At the age of forty-seven he gave up a life of chronic drunkenness and broke with his past in order to become a Baptist. He and his wife joined the Church in the summer of 1963. Immediately they became among the most active members of the congregation—so much so that within six months Nikolai Khmara was standing in front of a Soviet court with three others, accused for their religious activities and for not accepting the statutes of the All-Union Council. The trial took place from December 24–27. Pastor Subbotin, the leader of the congregation, was sentenced to five years' imprisonment and Nikolai Khmara to three.

But Brother Nikolai was not to serve his sentence. Two weeks later his wife received back his dead body. As the sentence had already been passéd, the murder cannot have been carried out during the stress of an investigation. Someone in the prison had tortured him to death in cold blood. There were burn marks on the palms of his hands, his toes and the soles of his feet. The lower part of his stomach had been punctured by the insertion of some sharp instrument, he had been beaten on his legs and ankles, which were badly swollen, and all over his body, which was covered in bruises. When his wife looked at his mouth, she noticed that it had a rag stuffed inside it. On removing it, she recoiled in horror. Her husband's tongue had been cut out. The details of this murder have been confirmed by a partial photographic record which has been published.[11]

These tragic events, coupled with the continuing arrests and news of others who were being brutally treated in prison, made the Christians feel that another Stalinist purge had descended upon them. Yet, far from giving up hope, they found their faith strengthened. They felt like the Christians in the catacombs. As one of the movement's poets (possibly Vins) expressed it:

And now blood flows again.
Siberia is a second Coliseum,
Dogs devour Odintsov,
The order is given, "Finish them off!"
Others have been tortured,
And that has happened elsewhere
Than in Kulunda, which witnessed recent murder—
Our dearest Brother Khmara sad struck down ...
Formerly they used to raise a church
Where the remains of martyrs lay interred.
What now have persecutions given us?
They bear new life to churches everywhere.

The answer of the believers to all these events was an action
of the most incredible bravery. Six weeks after the murder of
Khmara, in conditions of secrecy in an unknown place, there
opened the first All-Union Conference of Baptist Prisoners'
Relatives. Undoubtedly Vins and Kryuchkov played a big part
in reaching the decision to set this up. Later Vins's mother,
Lidia, was to play a leading role in its activities, which have
gone on unbroken now for over six years (at the time of writing),
despite the determined efforts of the whole Soviet police system
to break up the movement. It was primarily a women's activity,
in which those whose relatives had been arrested acted fearlessly
and unselfishly, with a love and concern of apostolic quality.
Polemics with the All-Union Council were to play no role.

It has been insufficiently realized that these remarkable
people were doing something quite new in a society under a
communist régime. Never before had such an organization for
the support of those in prison existed. In the painful though
inexorable progress towards a human rights movement which is
now occurring in the Soviet Union, these Baptists hold a place
of high honour. It is incomprehensible that their sterling devotion and unbelievable bravery should not have received
greater recognition than they have in the Christian West. Early
in 1968 certain Czechs and Slovaks set up an organization for
the rehabilitation of political prisoners, which was widely reported to be the first of its kind in a communist country. It was
not. Four years earlier the Russian Baptists were fighting for

T–D

the rights of prisoners under immeasurably more difficult circumstances.

We owe the bulk of the information which we have received since 1964 about the Russian Baptist reform movement to these people. From the first, they collected all the precise personal and juridical details about the prisoners whom they could locate. Immediately they gathered information on 155 prisoners. By the time they next met, on July 5, they knew of 197 prisoners of their own faith who had been sentenced since 1961. Twenty-two of these had already been released, but five (four others besides Nikolai Khmara) had died while in prison or under investigation. The Khmara incident, therefore, was not isolated, though it is by far the best documented. There were, then, at this time 170 known to be in prison, as well as a further four under investigation. Most had been sentenced to three or five years but thirteen had received from five to ten years. Together they had 442 dependants, of whom 341 were children. All these families were left without the support of the chief breadwinner. There is in Russia no national assistance or social security support for the dependants of prisoners. They work or starve. This Council of Prisoners' Relatives organized charitable relief from among more fortunate Baptists to compensate for the inhumanities of the Soviet system. Twelve children had been taken away from their parents completely because they were being brought up as Christians.

All the initiators of the Council of Prisoners' Relatives were soon themselves in prison, as the Soviet police hounded them out and widened their net to entrammel them. Nevertheless, as soon as one group was swept away another small band of leaders stepped forward to continue the brave work. They have kept us fully informed of all the details of the imprisonments ever since. They were the first to reveal the exact locations and postal addresses of many present-day Soviet labour camps.

Reviewing all this, it is hardly surprising to find that Vins and Kryuchkov considered the Soviet laws on religion to be thoroughly bad, both in theory and implementation. They considered that Christians were being discriminated against and persecuted for their faith alone. They set out to prove this and succeeded in doing so. On April 14, 1965, Vins and Kryuchkov

sent a letter to Leonid Brezhnev, in his capacity as chairman of
a committee which was drafting a new constitution. In this
document yet another side of the abilities of these leaders is
demonstrated. It is, of course, possible that these two men, who
alone signed the document, might have called in a competent
legal expert to help them, but there is no evidence that they did
so. With finesse and objectivity of a high calibre, they traced
the history of Soviet legislation on religion since the Revolution. This document is too long and technical to be included
here, but it may be found on pages 105–13 of *Religious Ferment in Russia*.[12] This is an outline of what it said.

The laws affecting religious activity are both imprecise and
ambiguous. Some may look all right on paper, but in practice
they are an instrument of persecution. As they now stand, they
deny Lenin's original ideal of the separation of Church and
State and the right of people to propagate their faith, as well as
to practise it themselves. The 'freedom of conscience' guarantee in the Constitution has twice been modified to make it deliberately ineffective, indeed to give protection to those very
people who wish to deny the principle. The main instrument of
oppression is the complicated religious law of 1929, which
dates, pointedly enough, from the time when Stalin was preparing to initiate the greatest purge in history. This law must
be repealed and the original sense of the Constitution restored.

\*        \*        \*

There had been a lull in the persecution around the time when
Khrushchev fell from office (the end of 1964). Some prisoners
were released at the end of their sentences and a few others
were freed under an amnesty. Vins and Kryuchkov might legit-
imately have hoped for better things. They had grounds for
feeling that the new administration might give Christians a fair
deal. They were certainly right to change the focus of their
campaign at this time from their unhappy relations with the
All-Union Council to the Soviet Government itself. Yet the
appeal of Kryuchkov and Vins remained unanswered and
totally ignored. Many innocent people were left in prison,

many children were in need, and no group of believers who had followed the reformers found it possible to gain registration and to worship legally. The commitment which Khrushchev had made to exterminate religion in all its visible forms by 1980 was not annulled.

When Kryuchkov and Vins received no reply to their letter, they sent others. They began systematically organizing emissaries of local congregations to go to Communist Party offices in their areas and hand over requests for justice. The leaders of the Reform Movement themselves began a series of attempts to gain personal interviews with senior government officials. Finally, they decided that a major demonstration was called for, in the hope that they might gain the attention both of the government and of the public. The Central Committee building in Moscow was chosen as the place ... We have already described in Chapter I what occurred on that historic day, May 16, 1966.

## NOTES

1. Macmillan, London, and Praeger, New York, 1970.
2. *Religious Ferment in Russia: Protestant Opposition to Soviet Religious Policy*. Macmillan, London, and St. Martin's Press, New York, 1968.
3. Kuzin, author of the attack against Aida in *Smena*.
4. Great Russian poet of the early nineteenth century.
5. Russian eighteenth century scientist.
6. Czech martyr of the fourteenth century.
7. See p. 114.
8. Summarized on p. 90.
9. Alexander Karev quoted this and three other lines from this poem in his report to the Baptist All-Union congress in Moscow on December 9, 1969 (*Fraternal Messenger* 2, 1970, p. 21).
10. See pp. 75–6.
11. *Christian Appeals from Russia*, following p. 80.
12. See note 2 above.

*Chapter V*

# THE TRIAL

## Congress of 1966

June, July, August, September. The summer days of 1966 were over and the short autumn had succeeded them. All these months Georgi Vins, Gennadi Kryuchkov and almost all their closest associates, who had been arrested together during or after the demonstration at the Central Committee building in May, underwent the peculiar rigours and mental torture of a Soviet pre-trial investigation. The mood of their supporters, who had lost all their principal leaders at one swoop of the State Security organizations, was grim but not despairing. Grim, because they had hoped for better things with the accession to power of the post-Khrushchev collective leadership. Not despairing, because, as one of the reform Baptists once said, persecution is endemic in Soviet society. Their grandfathers had sown the seeds of the faith and been persecuted under the Tsars; their fathers had been persecuted under Stalin; now it was their turn under Khrushchev and his successors. Already the laurel wreath of martyrdom was being prepared to hand on to their children in their turn. Throughout all this, however, God had given them strength and not failed them.

Throughout the autumn and early winter there was a series of trials, not reported in the Soviet press, which removed the Reform Baptist leaders one after the other. Thanks to the religious grape-vine, however, many of the believers knew that they were taking place. The Baptist leaders may have been led shorn to the slaughter, but they were far from being the dumb victims of which the Bible speaks. The incredible Council of Prisoners' Relatives, who seem to have become more highly organized and even braver after the arrest of Vins and his

friends, saw to it that these trials have become some of the best
documented episodes in recent Soviet history. Somehow, even
when admission to the trials was rigorously controlled by passes
and the halls were packed with specially selected hostile people
come to jeer, sympathizers of the accused got in—not just to
one, but to a whole series of trials. They compiled stenographic
records unbeknown to the court authorities. They wrote them
up later. The Council of Prisoners' Relatives collected them
and published them in carefully-produced clandestine booklets,
which were circulated from hand to hand.

Some of them eventually found their way abroad—extensive
reports, often verbatim, of the trials of Makhovitsky, Khorev,
Kryuchkov, Vins and others in several cities, consisting of well
over two hundred pages of documentation, are in the author's
files for these few months alone (not counting the mass of material relating to subsequent years). In this book we publish a
very small part of them only, but this will be the first time that
any of this material has appeared in English.[1] Naturally, we
shall concentrate on the trial of Vins and Kryuchkov, but
before we reach November 29, 1966, the day it opened in
Moscow, there was another significant event in the life of the
Russian Baptist Church which occurred in the same city. This
was the Baptist congress of October 4–7.

It is doubtful whether any other major Christian conference
of recent years has opened in such inauspicious circumstances.
The atmosphere in Baptist circles on October 4 was highly
charged and not at all conducive to any form of calm reflection
and reasoning. When the task ahead was to attempt a delicate
piece of reconciliation between two bodies in schism who had
indulged in mutual recriminations for over five years, understanding could be achieved only in favourable circumstances.

The very idea of trying to achieve reconciliation with men
who were not present, but who were being held in Soviet
prisons for acting according to their consciences, must have
seemed ludicrous to many who were present at the 1966 congress. Of course, not many there had actively collaborated with
the atheist authorities to bring about this sorry situation, but
not many, either, had taken the risk of trying to make some sort
of stand or gesture to prevent it.

Even granted the best will in the world on the part of those present, the possibility of a satisfactory outcome was torpedoed before the congress opened. The very morning upon which the delegates assembled for the inaugural ceremonies, one of the principal republican newspapers, *Pravda Ukrainy* ('Ukrainian Truth') reported the sentence of Iosif Bondarenko and N. K. Velichko to three years' imprisonment each and of three of their associates to shorter sentences. They were all among Vins's closest supporters, for they had been fellow-workers with him in the Kiev congregation. Iosif Bondarenko, twenty-nine years old at this time, was known as being one of the most zealous evangelists of his generation (the 'Billy Graham of the Ukraine', as he has been called in the West—a term scornfully repeated by the Soviet atheist press in December 1969). The newspaper could find nothing more specifically anti-Soviet in their conduct than allegedly 'trying to corrupt the minds of children, deterring them from school and setting them against society'. Actually, the sentence had been passed a few days previously and was probably already well known to a number of those present at the congress. Nevertheless, the deliberate publication of the news on the very day it opened can be regarded only as one of the most cynical terrorist operations of the Soviet security system in recent years.

The minds of some of those present may have gone back twenty years to the occasion where, in the Ukrainian town of Lvov, a synod met which supposedly represented the Ukrainian Eastern-Rite (Greek Catholic) Church. It proceeded solemnly to vote this Church out of existence—also knowing that priests who had already refused to conform had been sent off to labour camps and that the delegates' own families were threatened.

Why devise new methods of terror if there are old ones at hand which have proved their effectiveness in the past? That was probably the reasoning of the security apparatus. "Conform and stop your open letters, meetings, demands—or else!" This is precisely what was being threatened.

I think we should seriously ask ourselves whether the All-Union Council was right to proceed with the congress at all in the circumstances. After all, its main business was supposed to be to achieve unity with the followers of men who were at that very moment being carried away to labour camps.

The All-Union Council, realizing the appalling impression its conduct was giving (justly or unjustly) to a number of people abroad, published an English record of this congress, a direct translation of the bulk of the reports on it in the official *Fraternal Messenger* (No. 6, 1966). Unquestionably the Soviet Government was behind this enterprise of bringing out *Documents of Moscow 1966 All-Union Conference of Evangelical Christian-Baptists*, but its appearance is to be welcomed, for it gives the non-Russian-speaking foreigner a unique opportunity to acquaint himself with the point of view of those Baptists in the Soviet Union who have decided that the best course of action for Christians in their situation is to accept guidelines and laws on internal Church affairs laid down by the State.

The congress could not and did not produce the desired re-unification of the Baptist movement, not only because of the terrorist conduct of the security agencies, but also because the reformers were not properly represented at any level. Quite apart from the fact that the top leaders were in prison almost to a man, the All-Union Council repeated the old mistake of 1963 and did not let any unregistered congregation be represented (even though the requirement of registration for membership of the official Council had been dropped at the 1963 congress). The 711 delegates who attended were very largely in sympathy with the policies of the All-Union Council. Supporters of Vins and Kryuchkov could attend as guests, but few decided to, because at an early stage they could see how the dice were being deliberately loaded against them. In fact, two emissaries from the reformers did attend, but what they said goes unreported —even though this was perhaps the most important part of the conference.

Nevertheless, despite these strictures on its work, there was—surprisingly—some frank discussion by a small number of men who decided to re-align themselves with the All-Union Council. It was this which provided the main justification for the continuation of the congress.

Before their turn came to speak, these observers listened to a long report on Russian Baptist activities from Alexander

Karev, General Secretary of the All-Union Council (AUCECB), and saw the adoption of a new set of statutes. Let us give Karev the chance to speak for himself on the nub of the controversy. To avoid any possible misrepresentation, we use the official translation:

During the five years of its activity, the 'Council of Churches' has issued a great many messages, 'fraternal leaflets' and other documents in which an unprejudiced reader will be struck by the astonishing degree of self-projection and self-glorification. Without consulting the Church, it excommunicated a number of AUCECB workers from the Church, but from what Church? . . .

AUCECB repeatedly called on the 'Council of Churches' to settle all the misunderstandings that had arisen, but unfortunately, received more insults in reply . . . Regrettably, the 'Council of Churches' has not only refused to take part in the congress itself, but also called on its adherents to boycott it . . . We shall welcome any brother or sister who wishes to return to our ranks in order to glorify together our great Redeemer Jesus Christ.

We pray for our brothers and sisters from the 'Council of Churches' who have suffered through certain erroneous actions on their part and we hope that the authorities will show humanity and lenience to those who are at present in custody.

One can here detect an urgent desire for reconciliation, together with a determination in the last paragraph to do something about it. This accords ill, however, with the preceding statement that the leaders of the Reform Movement had 'refused' to take part in the congress—when Karev knew perfectly well that they were all in prison as he spoke.

The main defect of Karev's statement, however, is that, while sharply criticizing several aspects of the reformers' activities and seeking to place all the blame on them, he totally ignores the root cause of their complaint against the AUCECB—the adoption of the ill-omened *New Statutes* and *Letter of Instructions* in 1960. It is hard to see how there can be any genuine reconciliation until there has been a detailed explanation of precisely why this was done and who was behind it.

On the second day, the congress passed on to the adoption of an entirely new constitution. The unsatisfactory old format was dropped and the result looks much more like a Christian document. Again, there were direct concessions to the demands of the reformers. While not completely democratizing the appointment of senior presbyters (whose activities had in some instances appalled Prokofiev, Vins and Kryuchkov in the Khrushchev era) local opinion was given weight in their choosing. The new constitution mentioned the setting up of courses and seminars for ministers, preachers and choir trainers. When a correspondence course for pastors opened soon after, this was a major step forward for a Church which had had no such official training for nearly forty years (though six students had been able to complete two-year courses in England in the late 1950s). At the time of writing there is still no guarantee, however, that these courses will continue as a permanent institution, because their legal status is so insecure. However, over one hundred had enrolled by 1968 and it was hoped that this number would double. Also, three students came to London to study in 1967, but were recalled before they even had time to learn English. Two of them returned in 1970.

The most tense session of the congress was the third day. The full proceedings have never been reported. Brothers Ye. T. Kovalenko and G. I. Maiboroda addressed the congress on behalf of the reformers. They, at least, had not been intimidated by the threats of the Soviet authorities against them. The English version reports nothing at all of what occurred that day until the evening session, which began with a long report on unity by Brother S. P. Fadyukhin, Assistant General Secretary, which covered much of the same ground that Karev had done earlier. He did, however, refer to the 1960 *New Statutes* and *Letter of Instructions*, dealing with the traumatic crisis they had caused in the churches (especially in view of repeated statements by AUCECB officials that they were a yardstick of loyalty both to the Church and to the State) in these words:

They have not been approved by our Brotherhood and

have therefore been repealed. And in presenting a Statute, drawn up on the basis of the AUCECB draft approved by the 1963 congress, the AUCECB has, to the great joy and satisfaction of all God's children, proved sincerely and in humility that it is capable of producing and has actually produced fruit worthy of repentance.

This presumably means that the AUCECB now repents for having introduced the 1960 documents. Fadyukhin continued:

We also entertain a bright hope that with God's help and by the common effort of all God's children such phenomena, which sometimes occurred in the past, will be eliminated, as: ordaining protopresbyters (senior presbyters) without the consent of the church of which they are members, ordaining presbyters outside the church and without being elected by the church for which they were ordained, retention in service of protopresbyters and presbyters who had clearly lost their pastoral dignity and the respect of the children of God, as well as some other aspects that definitely fall under the heading of internal church affairs.

Fadyukhin was here going a very long way indeed to be conciliatory. Let there be no misunderstanding: 'ordaining presbyters outside the church' does not mean 'religious ceremonies on the village green'! It means 'government agents being insinuated for the destruction of the church'. This admission would have been amazing enough under any circumstances, let alone in the particularly distressing situation which we have described. It is highly unusual to find an official Soviet publication referring directly to the improper interventions of the security agencies.

These words alone were tantamount to an admission that many of the reformers' accusations—their whole movement even—had been justified. It is not known how representative an opinion Fadyukhin was expressing. In his pastoral duties at Tashkent he must have come very closely into contact with the reformers, who were very strong in his own particular area.

Undoubtedly he had come to see that there was much justice in what they were saying and he did not mince his words in revealing his attitude. In the Orthodox Church, no present administrator of the Moscow Patriarchate has ever spoken thus.

One of the major tragedies of the recent history of the Russian Baptists was that this olive branch was extended to people who were being physically prevented from reaching out their own hands to receive it. Indeed, Vins and Kryuchkov, at this point nearing the culmination of their pre-trial investigation, probably did not even hear about the conciliatory move for a considerable time. We have no proof that they heard about it at all before the end of their prison sentences nearly three years later. What would have happened if these overtures had been made before the demonstration of May 1966 and one or two of the All-Union Council officials had gone along to the Central Committee building with the reformers? It is useless to speculate, but very probably the schism would have been healed.

Not surprisingly, the bravery and forthrightness of Brother Fadyukhin's speech made a great impact on the small number of supporters of the Reform Movement who were present. The pity is that they were so few. More than a dozen people spoke on the matter under discussion, some of whom had already rejoined the official Church at some time in the past, some of whom were considering it now. Brother N. I. Vysotsky from Odessa said:

The first obstacle is the over-zealous adherents of the AUCECB. They are being more Catholic than the Pope, and they are prepared to call all dissenters 'the Devil's servants', 'children of Satan' and other unsavoury names. Such 'zealots' do nothing but harm to our Brotherhood, for this is not in the spirit of Christ. The second reason is inflexible, self-righteous clergymen. The AUCECB admits its errors, and it would be just as well for the 'Organizing Committee' to follow suit. We all have made mistakes, let us admit them freely at this congress, and this will accelerate our progress towards unity . . . A delegate from the Ukraine, speaking on the report by the AUCECB General Secretary, has sounded a note of grievance. He said: "Why should those who returned from the 'Organizing Committee' be elected to the office of protopresbyter? Haven't we got enough of our own men to fill the office?" Such utterances do not contribute to the cause of unity. Of course, this is the personal opinion of this particular brother from the Ukraine, and most of the delegates, I am sure, do not share this opinion.

Brother M. I. Azarov, from Belgorod in the Ukraine, attended in a private capacity as an observer who had been a loyal supporter of the reformers. He laid the blame for what had happened squarely on the shoulders, not of Prokofiev, Vins and Kryuchkov, but of "certain protopresbyters ordained by the AUCECB, who deserve to be called dire rather than dear". He went on to say that the senior presbyter of the Belgorod area had caused much harm to the Baptist faith and that there could be no question of unity until such people had been removed from office. He turned to Alexander Karev and asked three questions. He wanted to know whether the AUCECB would recognize the status of those who had been ordained as pastors, deacons and preachers within the Reform Movement; he asked whether the Church would from now on be guided by the Word of God and whether help would be offered to, and prayer on behalf of, those who were in prison. Karev answered 'yes' to all three questions and added that, as he himself had been in prison, he always prayed for those in similar circumstances. He added that all Christians were free to offer material help from their own personal budgets. Karev ended by regretting the discordant note which had been struck by Kovalenko and Maiboroda, but nevertheless his conciliatory answers to Azarov produced their effect.

On the final day of the congress there were elections to representation on the All-Union Council. Of the twenty-five chosen, at least one, V. F. Vasilenko, was known as a former supporter of the reform position, so here was a further attempt at reconciliation. However, those elected to the presidium, who are responsible for the day-to-day administration of central Baptist affairs, were all long-standing supporters of the official position (people whom, incidentally, the reformers had earlier decided to excommunicate).

*The Court-Room*

Georgi Vins and Gennadi Kryuchkov, at the very time when
they might save been using their influence to promote the new
cause of reconciliation, were instead being held incommunicado
in a Moscow prison. Already the Soviet press was whipping up
a hysterical atmosphere against the accused. On June 5, 1966,
the government newspaper, *Izvestia*, printed an article accusing a woman of the ritual murder of a child. It is dubious
from the text whether the woman was a Baptist. Yet Vins and
Kryuchkov were represented as inciting her religious fanaticism. The whole episode sounded like a fake.

The pre-trial interrogation neared its end and the stage was
being set for the biggest insult to the Reform Movement which
the State had paid it since its inception. It was as if one faction
among Soviet officialdom had decided that reconciliation was
the best way to be rid of this growing Baptist menace, which
seemed to be offering an increasingly direct challenge to Soviet
policies towards religion, while at the same time another faction had decided that even more severe repression was the only
way of bringing the leaders of the movement to heel. In the
event, both policies were tried simultaneously and the result
was a total failure from the State's point of view and a tragedy
from that of the Church—for there seems little doubt that, left
to its own devices and being free to seek its own spiritual guidance, the Russian Baptists would have been re-united into a
single strong movement at this point. Perhaps it was precisely
this which some policy-makers in the security agencies feared
most of all. 'Divide and rule' is a maxim of which they have
proved the worth time and time again in the pursuance of their
own goals.

Seven-and-a-half weeks after the conclusion of the congress,
on Tuesday, November 29, 1966, the curtain went up on one of
the most infamous, though least-reported, of trials in recent
Soviet history. We present this account of it in such detail for
two reasons: firstly, because these facts are not at present available anywhere else in any language; secondly, because it demonstrates in three dimensions and with unique vividness the
precise nature of the continuing Soviet persecution of religion.

In our description we shall keep faithfully to the facts as contained in the transcript before us and we shall use its actual words where possible. For the sake of brevity, some omissions will be made.

This is how the author of the transcript sets the scene:

Before the judical proceedings began, the court-room was filled with specially invited people—collaborators of the Council for Religious Affairs [the government body overseeing the Churches], people from the periodical *Science and Religion*, propagandists of atheism from the Society for the Dissemination of Knowledge, representatives of the press and others.

It was also impossible for friends of the accused, Baptist believers, to get into the court-room and only a few managed with great difficulty to do so.

First of all the judge asked whether Vins and Kryuchkov had any special requests to present to the court. Vins asked that his relatives and friends should be admitted to the hearing. He was also unhappy with the so-called 'experts' (men whose job it is to supply specialized background to the court in cases such as this). They knew nothing about theological matters, Vins said, and the documentation they had produced should be dismissed from the case. He went on to ask for the right to summon six defence witnesses (which had been denied him) and said he wished to conduct his own defence. He was going on to amplify his reasons for making these requests when the judge abruptly interrupted and turned to Kryuchkov, to ascertain whether he had any requests of the court.

Kryuchkov echoed several of Vins's pleas and added that two principal prosecution witnesses should be forced to appear in court. He also wanted precise statistics to be available to the court on such enforced closures of churches as were known to the Council on Religious Affairs.

The judge interrogated them as to why they had made these requests. Kryuchkov said it was essential that these defence witnesses should appear, otherwise the court would be dealing with hearsay testimony known only at third or fourth hand.

However, apart from being granted the right to dispense with defence lawyers, every single plea entered by the defendants was turned down (though the judge said he would give further consideration to the matter of the witnesses). Even Nadezhda, Georgi Vins's wife, and his mother were absent.

Vins was asked what he had to say in answer to the charges made against him (it was not clear at this point precisely what these were). Vins began by recounting the circumstances of his arrest, which are already familiar to us.[2] He went on to say that the charge against him had been trumped up and the real reason for his arrest was because he had been discharging his duty as a pastor of his church. At this point the proceedings were interrupted for the first of many times by derisive noises from the people hand-picked to be present in court precisely to present such a barrage of hostility to the defendants (conduct unknown in any country with a civilized legal system).

Vins went on to make a résumé of the history of the Reform Movement. The judge interrupted and allowed him to make no reference to the mass arrests of recent years: "You are charged with publishing literature and its mass distribution. Do you want to give the court an explanation?" Before he could do so, the judge turned to Kryuchkov.

We must at this point interpose a word about this charge. As stated here by the judge, the distribution of literature in the Soviet Union is not an offence. Even after the tightening of the law in March 1966 it became an offence only to produce or distribute leaflets or letters which "call for the infringement of the laws on religious cults". By implication, therefore, literature which made no such call was legal. The judge, to make any sense out of his charge, would have had to prove that the contents of this literature called for such an infringement.

Kryuchkov then stated that they were being tried on two further charges—setting up Sunday schools for children and organizing the delegation of May 16–17 to the Central Committee building. Only the first of these is in fact an offence under Soviet law, for the right to organize delegations and demonstrations is guaranteed by the Constitution.

Kryuchkov then went on to say that the aim of his religious organization was in no sense to breach Soviet legislation on religion. Indeed, the whole purpose of what he was doing was to redress the illegalities to which believers had been subjected: prayer houses had been removed, for instance, in Vladivostok, Chelyabinsk, Brest and many other places. They were demolished by bulldozers, roofs were taken off, meetings of believers were dispersed and private dwellings where meetings were being held were confiscated. Then the May 1961 decree on the campaign against parasitism came out. In the attached explanation there was, according to Kryuchkov, an indication of what kind of people could be prosecuted:

1) those engaged in begging;

2) people—I don't want to use the French term, so I will say it in Slavonic—harlots, women who lead immoral lives;

3) pastors of unregistered congregations.

... In the town of Dedovsk, Moscow Region, five people were arrested—I'll give their names: P. A. Rumachik, V. F. Ryzhuk, V. Ya. Smirnov, A. Kayukov and P. V. Alexandrov. They were arrested although they were all in employment.

*Judge:* Are you completely certain that they were all working?

*Kryuchkov:* Yes, I know for a fact that they were all in employment. Yakimenkov was arrested at his lathe in Novomoskovsk and sentenced as a parasite. Furthermore, Smirnov's house was confiscated, which was provided for under the decree ... In Odessa, the prayer house was handed over to a poultry farm as a club. I can continue this list *ad infinitum*, but I think the facts cited will suffice.

We believers, when we suffer such persecutions from others, even though they are not justified by law and are unconstitutional, have not shed tears and will never do so. We accept persecution from others as our due. But our religious leadership, the All-Union Council, has accepted a compromise with atheists by writing documents which limit the age of baptism, forbid children to be brought to worship and corrupt our young people.

Kryuchkov went on to review the programme of the reformers in their attempt to re-structure the Baptist movement
in the Soviet Union:

> The Organizing Committee began to petition the govern-
> ment for legal permission to hold a congress ... Altogether,
> about thirty declarations were sent by us to official depart-
> ments, but we did not receive a single reasoned reply.
>
> At this time we began receiving communications from
> Baptist believers in various towns and villages requesting
> that we should assume the leadership. The faithful accepted
> the Organizing Committee as their religious leaders. There
> were hundreds of such letters with thousands of signatures
> attached. We forwarded copies of them to government
> bodies ... These documents show that we are not impostors,
> but have been chosen by thousands of believers in our
> country. I was elected Chairman of the Council of Churches.
> Of this there can be no doubt, since it is proved by all the
> documents, although you have even refused to add them to
> the file on the case—but they're all in our files.

It is very important not only for our understanding of the
case, but also of the whole position of Kryuchkov, Vins and
their fellow-reformers, to note that this claim to leadership
which Kryuchkov made at this point was explicitly accepted
next day by the prosecutor, when he agreed that "they have
been elected and enjoy wide support among Baptists. They
certainly wield authority—that can't be denied."

By 7 p.m. on the first day the court had completed the interrogation of seven witnesses. There was no break for a
meal.

There was evidence from policemen and passers-by who had
seen the events at the Central Committee building. Four supporters of the Reform Movement were interrogated and put up
a spirited defence of their position—because of which there
were frequent indignant interruptions from the hostile hand-
picked observers in court, including demands that these witnesses should be put in the dock with the defendants. Here is an
example of the exchanges:

### Witness A. A. Gerbel (from Prokopievsk)

*Judge:* How many children have you?

*Witness:* Six.

*Judge:* Are you a member of a registered community?

*Witness:* An unregistered one.

*Judge:* Do you know the defendants?

*Witness:* No.

*Judge:* What have you heard about them?

*Witness:* They are my kin. (Laughter in court.)

*Judge:* How are they your kin?

*Witness:* My brothers in the blood of Jesus Christ.

*Judge:* You are seeing them for the first time. Why are you certain that they are your brethren?

*Witness:* Because they're in the dock.

*Judge:* What kind of organization is the Council of Churches?

*Witness:* That's an internal Church question.

*Judge:* Did you elect them?

*Witness:* Yes.

*Judge:* Were they in Prokopievsk?

*Witness:* Ask them.

*Judge:* Do you people teach religion to children?

*Witness:* Yes.

*Judge:* Do your children attend worship?

*Witness:* Yes.

After this packed day of almost nine hours of court proceedings, what happened next can hardly be credited under the Soviet or any other system of law. The judge insisted that the interrogation of Vins should begin. He naturally objected, saying that he would find it impossible to concentrate after such a gruelling day; he believed the attempt to exploit his exhaustion was deliberate. All his protests were overruled. A period of intensive interrogation began, which lasted almost five hours and did not end until nearly midnight.

Vins accepted that he was responsible for the literature which had been produced by his organization, but made the defence that there was nothing illegal in it. The early stage of the questioning, however, concerned not this but his part in organizing the May demonstration.

We have only the briefest record of this lengthy interrogation, but from what the compilers of the stenographic report wrote, it does not appear that any new facts of great significance came to light. Nor did any in regard to the literature of the movement, though very significantly the prosecution was unable to come up with any quotations which called upon believers to break the law or incited them to anti-Soviet activities.

Vins's testimony did not end until shortly before midnight. Both the defendants were awakened at five next morning, having been almost totally deprived of their night's sleep. Such was 'Soviet justice' forty-nine years after the Revolution!

By the beginning of the second day's hearing, word had spread among believers in Moscow what was afoot. Sympathizers arrived to find that the street approaches and the corridors of the court were thronged with police who were trying to prevent any sort of demonstration. In particular, they considered it imperative to keep all Baptists out of the court-room again. They had probably been told of an incident in Moldavia just previously when word had got around that a court case was in progress. Believers gained entry into the court-room and brought the trial to a complete halt by singing hymns as a sign of support for the accused. It was essential to avoid any such embarrassing incidents here in the capital city, where foreign journalists might hear of them and splash them over the newspapers of the world.

So from 9.30 a.m. all the specially selected people began once again to fill up the court-room. At 10 o'clock the proceedings re-opened and Kryuchkov and Vins again asked for their relatives and friends to be admitted. Their wives and Vins's mother were standing outside the door, but had been refused permission to enter.

At this point the judge allowed the closest relatives in, but none of the other believers who were with them. Vins's mother claimed that they should all come in, since the court-room had been empty when they arrived. The judge refused, so she and Kryuchkov's wife left the room as a protest, saying that they would return when a fair selection of the public was allowed to be present.

Even more serious was the absence of two witnesses, Grigorovsky and Shveikin, upon whose evidence the prosecution had built much of their case. Neither had the defence witnesses come whose presence had been requested by Vins and Kryuchkov the previous day. The defendants put in a strong plea to have the case deferred until the evidence could be properly assembled. There was a break for consultation on these points, but it was eventually stated that Grigorovsky's and Shveikin's depositions would be read and that the defence witnesses could not come. They were under detention and the court was too busy to wait until they could be rounded up and brought to Moscow.

The evidence of P. M. Shveikin, an old man of ninety-one, which was read to the court, was founded on nothing but hearsay. No court in a western democracy could possibly have admitted it:

Substantially, I can state the following. In April I did in fact attend a meeting in Tashkent where Khrapov was present. From him I heard that there had been a discussion at some meeting or other about setting up a Mothers' Council to petition the government for permission to give children religious instruction, and the question of a delegation was raised. The question of children was also discussed at a meeting in Kiev.

Kryuchkov and Vins now both made a stand and refused to testify any further until Khrapov, Shveikin and others were in court. The judge ignored their pleas and turned to the two 'experts' for their testimony—the 'experts' whose very place in the trial had already been contested by the defendants because they allegedly knew nothing about religion.

The 'experts' amply demonstrated just how right Kryuchkov and Vins were. The first set out to review the literature of the Reform Movement, but the best quotations he could produce to back up his accusation of anti-Soviet activity were on these lines: "There is a limit to subjection to human authority," which he interpreted as an ultimatum to the State! From such passages the 'expert' built up the case that the whole thrust of the Reform Movement was a campaign to abrogate Soviet laws. The second concluded that as there were no dogmatic differences between the reformers and the All-Union Council the question must be one of politics. Therefore, since the latter had made an accommodation with the régime, the reformers must be against it. To refute this allegation, Kryuchkov requested that the letter he had written to the Constitution Commission[3] should be read out to the court. His request was refused.

Vins pointed out that the court, instead of trying them, was deliberately wearing down their physical resistance. He entered a plea to have the record of his interrogation the previous night erased, since he had been totally unable to concentrate because of his physical exhaustion. Naturally, the request was refused, but the judge did allow a break for the defendants to be served a hot meal.

Upon the resumption, the prosecutor made his main speech. He picked out for especial abuse the glorification of suffering which is allegedly found in the literature of the Movement, saying that this proved that its main aim was to persuade people to set themselves against Soviet laws and challenge them directly. He was especially critical of the fact that the émigré newspaper, Posev, had published some of the documents of the reformers. He thereby maliciously created the false impression that the reformers were connected in some way with people working outside the country for the overthrow of the Soviet régime. Of course he produced not one whit of evidence for the allegation, nor any objective appraisal of the policies of the N.T.S. ('National Labour Union'), which publishes Posev. He concluded his case with these words:

> Kryuchkov describes as heroes people who, in defiance of the law, give instruction to small children. This attitude of his towards transgressors of the law is particularly scandalous.
>
> Kryuchkov and Vins are well aware of the ideology that dominates our society—one that has nothing in common with religion. Yet, in spite of our ideology and in spite of what is taught in the schools, they go and organize religious instruction for children.

Comrade Judges! I consider that the charges made against Vins and Kryuchkov have been fully proven. The conclusions of the 'experts' report are just. Their crimes are correctly classified under Article 142, Part II, of the Penal Code of the Russian Republic.

It was then the turn of Georgi Vins to make his defence speech. He began by deploring the absence of the key witnesses:

The court can't objectively weigh and correctly decide for what reason and by whom the delegation to Moscow was organized, without the witnesses Yakimenkov, Baturin, Khrapov, Kozlov and Zakharov. One would think that the believers had nothing else to do than leave their jobs and families, spend money on travelling to Moscow, merely in order to hold a religious service at the Central Committee building of the Communist Party. No one has put the question why so many representatives of the congregations gathered in Moscow. Neither the 'experts', nor the prosecutor, nor the assembled court made any attempt even to establish the real reason which led them to do this. I know that out of more than four hundred people only one joined the delegation haphazardly. He had come from the Odessa region on a shopping expedition, met the believers and joined up with them ... All the others were appointed by congregations and travelled to Moscow for a definite purpose ... The real reason was the incessant persecution ...

We believers have a great love and respect for freedom. We respect the freedom of local churches and of individual members. The Council of Churches has no power to command or give orders. It carries out what it is instructed to do by the Church and is answerable for this ...

The delegates travelled to Moscow not in order to conduct a religious service here: they came with their requests. They should have been received and listened to, but they were laughed at, as one delegate recounted. The believers were beaten up; some were sent to prison, others were despatched to their own towns, but they were given no positive reply to their justified and lawful demands ...

Baptist believers are still experiencing the same difficulties as they were. The problems about which they appealed to the government—the facts of persecution and repression—are excluded by everyone in this court.

Vins then turned to the testimony of the 'experts'. He put forward a most cogent argument that the objectives of the Reform Movement were not political, but the strictly religious ones of purity, sanctity and unity within the Baptist community. Before he had got very far, he had to contend with a mounting uproar from hostile people gathered for this purpose in the court. Against this he tried to make himself heard, but with no help from the judge. Vins went on:

I notice that there is a Bible lying on the table of one of the 'experts'. Surely this doesn't have to be the subject of an 'expert's' report? His descriptions of sins were taken from the Bible, but it is not under accusation today, you know, as a book which calls for disobedience to Soviet laws.

The 'experts' have made a mistake. The words, "Friendship of the world is enmity with God", constitute a crime in their view. The actual meaning of these words taken from the Epistle of St. James is that it is necessary to love God and not to love anything which estranges one from Him.

I consider it wrong for the 'experts' to intervene in the sphere of theology. These matters are not subject to court jurisdiction and the prosecutor is right in saying that he doesn't want to interfere in the realm of our faith. I don't claim that he hasn't been doing just this, but it's correct to say that there should be no interference in matters of belief.

We say that the Church should be subordinate only to Christ, and that is why we are being blamed. Theologically speaking, the Church has existed throughout the ages, and the sense of those words is purely theological.

The local congregations are a different matter. They may be registered and their executive body, being in charge of economic problems (property and buildings), may be controlled by the State. The congregation itself, however, as a Church, must be subordinate to Christ alone ...

Citizen Judges! We have had no occasion to exercise our rights. We have asked that literature not bearing the signature of the Council of Churches be removed from the case file—we were refused. We've asked that the findings of the 'experts' be dropped—refused. We've petitioned for witnesses to be summoned—also refused. Doesn't it look as if all believers' petitions are disregarded? In appearing before a court of the Russian Federation, I thought that my case would be examined in detail, and relevant matters penetrated in depth. You, however, have galloped through the whole trial.

Because the case has been heard at such a headlong speed, we have been placed in a difficult situation. The court has not been able to consider the case objectively.

It was then the turn of Gennadi Kryuchkov to deliver his defence speech. He protested strongly that his preparations for this had been made under the assumption that the witnesses whose presence he had requested would by this time have given their evidence. Now that they had not been summoned, he needed time to reorganize completely what he had been going to say. He therefore asked for an adjournment until the next afternoon. Although it was by this time 7 p.m., the judge refused even to consider an adjournment until the next morning. The following exchange then took place:

*Kryuchkov:* There has been a considerable rearrangement. Seven witnesses on whom I wanted to rely are not present. I now have to reconstruct my defence. You're in a hurry. Yesterday you were in a hurry, today you're in a hurry. You haven't produced the witnesses. It would suit you if I made no defence speech at all.
*Judge:* That's your right.
*Kryuchkov:* I consider that the working day is over. Only today you informed us that there would be no witnesses. The substance of the indictment consists of sixty pages, thirty of them being the 'experts' report. For its study you have al-

lotted the most restrictive time-limits laid down by law. You've not complied with a number of our petitions. Everything we've insisted on you've refused. As a consequence of all this, it is essential for me to reconstitute my defence.

*Judge:* There will be a break of fifteen minutes. We will discuss all the possibilities.

*Judge (after the break):* The court has decided to continue the hearing.

*Prosecutor:* I must state that the arguments advanced by the defendant regarding witnesses haven't been sufficiently proven and the requests he has submitted are not fundamental. I consider that the hearing must be continued without delay. I've no time tomorrow. I have to take part in another case.

*Kryuchkov:* Are all cases decided in this way, then? Today you're hurrying off to one court, tomorrow to another. Will it be the same there? Because you're in a hurry, you'll be depriving people of the possibility of defending themselves. I'm not in a condition now to concentrate. The court has left a large number of questions untouched.

*Judge:* If you're unable to defend yourself, remember you were offered a defence counsel, but you refused. You said you were prepared to conduct your own defence.

*Kryuchkov:* I shall speak in my own defence, but at the moment I can't concentrate. I've tried, but it's very difficult. We had to get up at five this morning and it's now seven in the evening. I request an adjournment of the hearing.

*Judge:* You were given a hot meal today.

*Kryuchkov:* That's not what we're talking about. I need time to prepare my defence plea. You make a break when *you* need it.

Nevertheless, the judge did make a short break, after which Kryuchkov was obliged to present his defence. He began by pointing out strongly that the main prosecution case rested on hearsay evidence by witnesses who had not even been brought to the court. Petitions which had quite simply requested the right of parents to bring up children in their own religious faith were being represented as a demand for the abrogation of the

law on the separation of Church and State and the ending
of atheist education in schools. Further, the request that
the Council of Churches should call its supporters together
for a congress was an entirely legal one, seeing that only
internal church problems would be discussed. Kryuchkov went
on:

The prosecutor has stated that the Council of Churches
has been supporting unregistered congregations—and this is
regarded as a crime. The unregistered congregations were
unregistered even before the Action Group was formed.
They were so, not because of the setting up of this movement, but because the authorities refused to register them.
Even before the formation of the Action Group, there were
three thousand unregistered congregations (three times the
number of registered ones) . . .

The Council of Churches is not against registration provided the law is observed. However, the local churches fear
registration like the plague, because it has led to unlawful
interference by atheists in Church life. It was therefore very
hard for us to prove that it was necessary to register. In the
*Fraternal Leaflet* we wrote: "We have no right to refuse to
be registered."

Unlawful registration is another matter. If the authorities
are going to say that such and such a person may be a pastor,
but this other one not, that such and such a person is fit to
serve, but this other one not, and so on, then this is unlawful
registration. If we're going to be told how to conduct divine
worship, we cannot accept registration on such conditions:
no laws and no court will prove to me that I must accept such
registration.

We've been accused of using such words as, "The Church
is separated from the State." It has never been stated either
in God's word or in the law that the Church must be subject
to the State authorities. I'm prepared to accept responsibility
for that sentence. I see a dictionary on your desk. Look up
the meaning of the word 'Church'. The Church is a religious
organization. The State has no juridical right to control it.
The Church is completely separate. Where is it written in

the law that the Church should submit to the State authorities?

We want there to be controls. We're not in favour of an-
archy. If I commit an offence as a citizen, I can be held
responsible as an individual, but the State should not interfere in Church activities and my ministry should not be subject to such controls . . .

Kryuchkov went on to deny that he and Vins had organized
the May delegation to the Central Committee building:

I can say one thing: that delegation of believers was not
the first. I can't tell you precisely whether it was the fifth or
the seventh, but it wasn't the first. The first delegation was
from Barnaul, which surprised us greatly. No one knew of it,
no one organized it, no one called it into being. What could
have induced the believers to leave their work and travel to
Moscow? That delegation came here because several believers had been sentenced, one of them, Khmara, had died in
prison, the church building had been destroyed and they
were not being allowed to meet for worship. People were
coming to break up meetings with loudspeakers, fines were
being levied and the faithful were being persecuted at their
work. After all this the believers sent a delegation to
Moscow.

There was also a delegation from Kazan. The Council of
Churches knew nothing about it. There were also delegates
from Bryansk, Magnitogorsk and Belorussia. There was no
master-plan behind them. The Council of Churches heard
about the delegations only later.

When prisoners were released, they met and decided to go
and plead for their brethren who were still in prison. The
first delegation of ex-prisoners was a small one—only
twenty-two in all. The second one numbered a hundred from
all over the country.

No one has proved the involvement of the Council of
Churches in the delegation to the Central Committee on
May 16–17. We ask you to produce the people who were in
the delegation—they will tell you who was in charge of them.

You just don't want to hear them give evidence . . . It was the act of the believers themselves—an organized act, of course. If the Council of Churches had undertaken such an assignment, it could have collected together three thousand or more. We could have given someone a real surprise if we had wished!

We are blamed because in No. 7 of the *Fraternal Leaflet* we wrote: "We salute our brother and sister workers who duplicate our fraternal messages and appeals . . . We salute all who have been brought to court." We're told that by saluting those who have been in prison, we're thereby encouraging them to commit fresh breaches of the law.

Everyone can make his own judgment on this. I will say that if the State has rehabilitated one hundred and fifty of our brethren, then we're entitled to offer them flowers. You can reproach us for what you like, but not for that . . .

We do salute those who duplicate our literature. After all, it does not contain appeals to break the law, and we can salute those who distribute it. Even if it were printed in hundreds of millions of copies, this would still not be a criminal offence. As citizens of the Soviet Union, the law on the freedom of the press applies to us. It is untrue to say that we salute transgressors of the law.

Because of persecution, a situation has come about in which it is impossible to comply with the law. For example, the 1929 law forbids believers to offer one another material assistance. Can we comply with that? If our brethren have been unlawfully sentenced and have left behind them five, six or more children, can we leave them without help and expose them to the danger of physical emaciation?

Article 127 of the Penal Code of the Russian Republic reads: 'To leave people in danger is a crime.'

At this point, renewed bedlam broke out in court. It was so noisy that Kryuchkov asked for a break in the proceedings and the judge granted it for half-an-hour.

Upon the resumption, Kryuchkov again asked for literature not signed by the Council of Churches to be removed from the indictment. He went on:

I must tell you that the Council of Churches doesn't even know all the places where the literature is printed. The method of doing it is very simple—I knew it while I was still a child. You take gelatine, glycerine and glue, mix them all together and pour the solution out on to glass. Then you make an impression. Any girl or boy who wants to do something to serve God can do it. I'll tell you that dozens of believers use this method to publish literature, about which the Council of Churches sometimes knows nothing whatsoever. The Council of Churches tries to bring some kind of order into the publication of this literature. We had no desire to follow an illegal path. We have asked permission to have an office and to publish literature.

Once again the proceedings were interrupted by a chaotic noise. Kryuchkov begged the judge to attempt to impose some order on those present.

He went on to complain about the illegal searches of his and other people's premises for this literature. On one occasion the police terrified his eight children when they turned everything in the house upside down, but they found nothing. Another time they broke in to carry out a search. By now, Kryuchkov was so tired that he could go on no longer. The following exchange took place:

*Kryuchkov:* I haven't finished; I haven't summed up. I'm very tired. I ask you to adjourn the hearing until tomorrow. I'm getting confused.
*Judge:* Surely you've said everything?
*Kryuchkov:* I know best whether or not I've said everything. I can't continue now—I'm exhausted. Or do you want me to collapse here? I request that the rest of my defence speech be adjourned until tomorrow. I can no longer speak. I'm feeling very unwell now. I just can't go on talking.
*Judge:* We can't defer the case until tomorrow. We haven't got the time.

Instead of making any allowances for Kryuchkov, the judge abruptly turned to Georgi Vins and told him that it was now his turn to present his 'final address' (the right of every person under trial in a Soviet court). It was already very late at night.

### FINAL ADDRESS OF BROTHER G. P. VINS.

I want to say that I consider myself fortunate to be able to stand here and testify that I'm in the dock as a believer. I'm happy that for my faith in God I could come to know imprisonment, that I've been able to prove and strengthen myself. I do not stand here as a thief, a brigand or as someone who has infringed the rights of another person. I stand before you with a calm and clear conscience; I have honourably obeyed all the civil laws and faithfully respected the laws of God.

I thank God that I've been able to experience the great joy of hearing a witness from Siberia say that he considered me his brother in the blood of Jesus Christ. After this recognition I'm prepared to accept any sentence passed by the court.

In the presence of my wife, I want to offer thanks to God that He has revealed to me the truth of the teaching of Jesus Christ and that I am a Christian. I am glad that for two days I've been able to speak before all these people. Some of you hadn't the patience to hear us out—there were grins, laughter and noise.

I do not see you, Comrade Judge, Comrade Prosecutor and all here present, as my enemies; you're my brothers and sisters in the human race. When I leave the court-room, I shall pray to God for you there in my cell, asking that He should reveal His divine truth to you and the great meaning of life. (Shouting and laughter in Court.)

But here, too, there are my brothers and sisters in the blood of Jesus Christ. You are dear to me. The Bible alone has been my preceptor; it has taught me to be upright. For us Christians no prisons are needed.

*Judge (interrupting)*: By law one should not interrupt a defendant when he's delivering his final address, but you're delivering a sermon, you know. Don't forget what audience you're addressing.

*Vins:* I consider that in my final speech I must be given the opportunity of expressing all that's in my heart. In conclusion, I want to say:

> Not for robbery, nor for gold
> Do we stand before you.
> Today here, as in Pilate's day,
> Christ our Saviour is being judged . . .
>
> Once again abuse resounds,
> Again slander and falsehood prevail;
> Let He stands silent, sorrowfully
> Looking down on us poor sinners.
>
> He hears the sorry threats,
> He sees the trepidation of those people,
> Whose hands have gathered tears
> Of children, wives and mothers.
>
> Forgetful of history's lessons,
> They burn with desire to punish
> Freedom of conscience and of faith
> And the right to serve the Lord.
>
> No! you cannot kill the freedom of belief,
> Or imprison Christ in jail!
> The examples of His triumphs
> Will live in hearts He's saved.
>
> A silent guard binds round
> The friends of Christ with steel ring,
> But Christ Himself inspires us
> To stand serene before this court.
>
> No rebel call has passed our lips,
> No children offered as a sacrifice;
> We preached salvation constantly,
> Our message one of holy thoughts.

We call upon the Church of Christ
To tread the path of thorns,
We summon to a heavenly goal,
We challenge perfidy and lies.

And so we stand before you,
Or rather, have been forced to come,
So you can learn the ways of God,
That sons of His stay true to Him.

Fresh trials now and persecution
Will serve alone to strengthen faith
And witness God's eternal truth
Before the generations still to come.

At this point, uproar broke out in court once again, but this time the judge took it upon himself to quell it. He gave Vins no chance to continue, however, and turned to Kryuchkov to make his final address.

### FINAL ADDRESS OF BROTHER G. K. KRYUCHKOV

I summon up my last remaining strength.

You beat up four hundred people[4] outside the Central Committee building of the Communist Party. Multiply the four hundred delegates by the four hundred congregations which sent them. To beat up four hundred delegates means spitting in the face of the thousands of believers who sent them.

Those brethren who are at this moment in prisons and camps are suffering, not for having broken Soviet law, but for having been faithful to God and His Church. They're suffering for Christ, who called them to a new life. Some of them are reformed criminals. Thanks be to God that this was when they were of the world, but when God touched their hearts they selflessly followed after Him. Now they are ready to give up what is their own, but not to appropriate what belongs to others. (Uproar in court.)

You've no patience at all to listen.

I'm happy to stand before you as a Christian. I'm glad

that the court has not proved we've committed any offences, so if you observe the law we shall be liberated from imprisonment at once. But if you act in accordance with the prophecy of Jesus Christ about His followers, "They will also persecute you", then we shall be sentenced.

(Complete chaos in the court. Shout from the public: "Under what authority does this court come? Carry out either Soviet law or Christ's prophecy!")

We say that one must be selfless and not fear jeering and scorn. But it's not only a question of jeering. We're being thrown into prison and we must act so that our words correspond to our deeds.

This court hearing has astonished me, but I'm glad to be associated with the company of those who've gone to prison.

The compiler of the transcript of the trial ends with these laconic words, which sum up in a few sentences the quality of the justice which was administered that day:

The court proceedings ended at 1 a.m.

The court sentenced Brother G. K. Kryuchkov and Brother G. P. Vins to three years' imprisonment to be served in 'special régime' camps.

The following day the friends of the defendants went to the City Court and ascertained that the prosecutor and the judge were having a day off, although during the hearing the prosecutor had asserted that the case could not be adjourned until the next day, as he was in a hurry to be at another trial.

## NOTES

1. For the text of a trial at Odessa, see *Russian Christians on Trial*, published by the European Christian Mission, and obtainable from the Centre for the Study of Religion and Communism (see pp. 190–2).
2. See Chapter I.
3. See pp. 98–9.
4. Other documents say five hundred people. Kryuchkov, in prison, would have had no chance to check his figures.

*Chapter VI*

# PRISON

*Lidia and Nadezhda Vins*

'Soviet justice' had done its worst. Georgi Vins and Gennadi Kryuchkov had received the maximum sentence under the relevant article of the Penal Code. But that was just about the only legally normal aspect of the trial. It was conducted before a public gallery baying for the blood of the defendants, and set out to do little less than render the accused physically incapable of defending themselves. The verdict was brought in at one o'clock in the morning. Such is the lot of the Christian in the Soviet Union today who will in no way compromise his faith.

All the other leaders of the Reform Movement and very many of their most prominent sympathizers were sentenced at about the same time. We have the trial transcripts of a few others, and from these we can see that the treatment meted out to Vins and Kryuchkov was no better and no worse than the others received, except that not everyone was given the maximum sentence. Hundreds of these people are no more to us than names on a list, but they were not forgotten by their friends, relatives and sympathizers left behind.

Nadezhda Vins watched her husband being led away from the dock. He disappeared from sight, but he and Kryuchkov did not disappear from the minds of those who continued to pray for them during the long imprisonment ahead. Indeed, those sentenced provided a source of inspiration for the future activities of those still free.

Nadezhda Vins was left to cope with four children of school age. This would have been a difficult enough task, even if she had continued to earn her former good salary as a highly qualified translator of foreign languages. But, according to the usual Soviet practice, punishment was extended to the relatives of the convicted man. She lost her job and had to take up a menial task. When she found employment as an ice-cream seller, she probably reflected wryly that at least this did not cut her off from contact with children. She doubtless also helped her mother-in-law, with whom she lived, to publicize the case of her husband and his fellow-sufferers and fighting for the justice for which they had sacrificed their freedom.

With this new wave of arrests in 1966–7, the emphasis of the Reform Movement now shifted away from arguments with the official organization, the All-Union Council of Evangelical Christians and Baptists. It also partly shifted from the direct approaches which had been made to the State in an attempt to secure justice. Some of these were continued, even though doing so had caused so much trouble for Vins and his associates.

Now, however, the perspective was to be widened at the same time as the issue itself was narrowed. The primary aim became that of proving a series of violations of elementary human rights to the court of world public opinion, as represented by U Thant and the United Nations Organization. Having failed to persuade the Soviet Government to redress their grievance, the reformers now had to fight for the rights of those who had been imprisoned unjustly and, at home, to organize relief for those families who were suffering so bitterly through the loss of their breadwinner.

We have already pointed out the significance of the Council of Prisoners' Relatives, which had been set up at an earlier stage of the Reform Movement's existence. Some prime movers of this Council had been present at the Moscow demonstration of May 1966. They were obviously high on the 'wanted' list of the security agencies, who must have regarded their existence as one of the most threatening aspects of the Reform Movement. The majority of those who had been rounded up after the demonstration were released a few days later, when preliminary interrogations and investigations had been conducted. But those connected with the Council of Prisoners' Relatives were, like Vins and Kryuchkov, tried and sentenced.

A new group of women banded themselves together to lead

the Council. Among them were Lidia Vins, Nina Yakimen-kova, Alexandra Kozorezova, Klavdia Kozlova and Yelizaveta Khrapova, all of whom had recently seen close relatives disap-pear into labour camps. They launched themselves into a period of intense and courageous activity.

They addressed a whole series of appeals to U Thant and the United Nations in 1967-8. In order to back up their case, they collected together a great dossier of facts about the religious situation in the U.S.S.R. In doing so, their movement broad-ened out from the narrowly religious sphere into many other realms. For example, no one else has compiled such an exten-sive list of prison camps, together with their exact locations and addresses. Every student of the Soviet legal system will want to be acquainted with the transcripts of the Baptist trials. Socio-logists, after this, cannot fail to give due weight to the significance of sectarian movements (and religion in general) in Soviet society.

The information which Lidia Vins and her friends have pro-vided is so detailed that it would be quite superfluous to do much more in the rest of this chapter than reproduce what they say. The facts themselves provide all the arguments we need at this point—though we should mention that a very great deal must simply be omitted for space reasons.

The most important single task which Lidia Vins and her group accomplished was the compilation of up-to-date lists of prisoners. By the second half of 1968 there were no less than 223 names on the list, nearly all of whom had been sentenced since the beginning of 1966. Some of these were released in 1969 at the end of their sentences, but new arrests followed. Adding all these to the names on the lists compiled during the first wave of arrests in 1962-4, then, we know of over five hundred sentences carried out against supporters of the Baptist Reform Movement during the first eight years of its exist-ence.

Each new list is more detailed than the last. There is a recent one which summarizes the situation in the second half of 1968, giving the following precise details for the great majority of the prisoners: full name, year of birth, precise date of arrest, article of the Penal Code under which sentenced, length of sentence,

precise home address, number of dependent relatives and
address of the prison camp. In many instances, even the next of
kin is given, so that the brethren know precisely to whom they
may offer relief. At least seventy-five prison camps are designated. This in itself is massive corroboration of the continued
existence of the Stalinist labour camp system, which was described by Anatoli Marchenko in *My Testimony*, memoirs of his
own experiences in the camps during the years 1960–6. A further list of November 1969 gives the nationality of many of the
prisoners, as well as the addresses of even more prison
camps.

What is perhaps most interesting of all is the age-range of
those sentenced. Kryuchkov was forty and Vins thirty-eight at
the time of their arrest in 1966. Of the 212 whose ages are
given in the 1968 list, seventy-three were born between 1917
and 1929 and no less than seventy-one in the decade 1930–9.
Twenty-two were born in the 'forties and were therefore in
their twenties or under when they were sentenced. One girl,
Raisa Burmai, from Chervonoarmeisk in the Ukraine, was born
in 1950 and was a mere seventeen when she was arrested in
January 1968, together with her sister who was a year older
than herself. In all, then, no less than 167 out of 212 grew up in
the post-revolutionary era, when religion was supposed to be
rapidly dying out in Soviet society, and only 45 were born
before the 1917 Revolution.

All this more than confirms the words of two of the most
prominent (and objective) Soviet atheist writers on religion,
A. I. Klibanov and L. N. Mitrokhin, when they stated in an
article, 'Schism in the Modern Baptist Church', published in
*Questions of Scientific Atheism*, Vol. III:

> They [the reformers] have been trying to impose their
> views on young people, to create something in the way of
> Sunday schools and youth seminars. In the milieu of those
> Baptists who come under the influence of the 'action group',
> young people are more numerous than in the other Baptist
> congregations. Sometimes supporters of the 'action group'
> have been forthrightly called 'young Baptists'. Over half of
> some of these groups consisted of young people.

To find such an admission in a published Soviet source is little short of amazing. We may consider as fully corroborated the evidence which we find in the Reform Movement's documents about the number of young people who belong to it; the testimony which we have about the age of the prisoners does not stand in isolation.

It must be rather galling for the leaders of the All-Union Council to find that their policies have led to less success with young people (although they have recently managed to institute successful youth choirs in some areas). For the Soviet régime, however, this must be an even more difficult pill to swallow. In this context, it is amusing to read continuing protestations in atheistic books and newspaper articles that 'religion with us is dying out—only the old and uneducated are interested now.'[1] This is the very opposite of the truth, as serious students of the atheist situation like Klibanov and Mitrokhin well know, and the Reform Movement among the Baptists is the best proof of this.

Lidia Vins and her friends were not content simply to send detailed lists of prisoners to the United Nations; they also dealt with many other ways in which human rights were being violated. Of three major documents which they sent to U Thant in 1967, we produce here extracts from one alone, dated June 5. We have space for less than a quarter of the full text, but we refer readers to the letter of August 15, 1967, printed in full in the recent book, *Christian Appeals from Russia*, pp. 33–59.

TO THE GENERAL SECRETARY OF THE U.N.O., U THANT . . .

> Copies to COMRADE L. I. BREZHNEV, GENERAL SECRETARY OF THE CENTRAL COMMITTEE OF THE COMMUNIST PARTY OF THE SOVIET UNION;

and to THE COUNCIL OF THE BAPTIST WORLD ALLIANCE . . .

*Kidnapping in the street*
Apart from the fact that believers are arrested at prayer meetings, at places of work and at home, the authorities have resorted to kidnapping them on the street, even though they have no prosecutor's warrant with them. This contradicts not only the 'Convention of Human Rights' (Article 9), but even

the fundamental law of our country, the Constitution of the U.S.S.R. (Article 127). Only subsequently is the prosecutor's sanction for the arrest obtained. The following, among others, have been seized in this manner: A. S. Goncharov and S. G. Dubovoi, members of the Council of Churches; Baptist believers L. D. Ovchinnikov (Kursk), Valentina Demina (Novomoskovsk, Tula region), L. A. Lepeshkin (Tula), N. P. Nechai (Sumy), Pyotr Peters (Perm), of whose whereabouts we have had no news to this day, and others. Only after a prolonged search do the relatives of those who have vanished discover the prisons where they are held.

## Analysis of the trials of believers

... The following extract from the indictment of V. A. Golub, N. I. Butkov and A. N. Balatsky, confirmed by the prosecutor of Lugansk on March 26, 1966, demonstrates why believers are imprisoned: "Golub, Balatsky and Butkov, in their sermons at the prayer meetings which are held two or three times a week, directly inspire belief in God and in the 'blessing' of the afterlife. In this they influence not only adult members of the Church, but minors also—schoolchildren who have been dragged in by them. They also instil in them that earthly life is transitory and that it is necessary to live according to the Biblical doctrine: 'All things are lawful unto me, but all things are not expedient.' Real life begins only after death ... In order to make children interested in attending church, the leader (Butkov) teaches children to play musical instruments, to the accompaniment of which they rehearse and perform religious hymns (Case History No. 138, pp. 1–2). For doing all this Golub, Balatsky and Butkov have been sentenced to four years in a normal-régime corrective labour camp ..."

We include in the text of our letter one incident which cries to heaven about the inhumanity of the Soviet authorities. It concerns the Christian invalid women from Tashkent, N. Matyukhina and M. Belan, as recorded at their trial on November 30, 1966.[2] The final address of N. P. Matyukhina, whose legs are both amputated above the knee, was as follows:

"What is humanitarian conduct? It is a very tender feeling of pity, sympathy and mercy; our socialist State is the most humanitarian in the world. I'm not judging society as a whole, but certain representatives of the government. For example, Investigator Dyachenko of the Lenin District, Prosecutor Khakimov, who authorized the arrest, and the local city prosecutor, Nikitin, have shown the presence of 'humanitarian feelings.'

"Both they and other representatives of authority well knew my physical condition, and they were not unfamiliar with prison conditions; they knew I would need help to fulfil my natural body functions. Nobody had prepared a stool for me in the toilet and there was no mat spread in the bathroom. In order to get to the wash house, I had to drag myself several yards along the cold cement floor and wash on a similar floor which was filthy.[3] Thanks be to God, I've not yet contracted any terrible disease, for all sorts of other people go to the same place to wash. After washing and before I could dress, I had to drag myself again several yards along that same dirty cold floor, getting covered with filth; then I had to dry myself on a damp rag and dress. Praise be to God that more humanitarian feelings are found among criminals, for they risked their health to protect mine, sometimes carrying me in their arms from the bathroom.

"Yes, the judicial authorities experimented in a very unfortunate way in picking on two cripples. You've made a great mistake ... but you can rest assured that our fellow-believers, far from being intimidated, would sooner join us here in the dock than try to flee into the woods before it's too late.

"Christ says, 'Blessed are ye, when men shall revile you and persecute you, and shall say all manner of evil against you falsely for My sake.' I will end my final address with this text:

In suffering for Christ no shame is ours,
But honour, glory He bestows.
To those who suffer here and now
Salvation comes as His good news.
                                        Amen ..."

*Believers tortured*

URGENT COMMUNIQUE TO THE GOVERNMENT FROM THE
KIEV BAPTIST CONGREGATIONS

With deep sorrow we inform you that on Thursday, March
20, 1967, we gathered for worship in the house of our fellow-
believer, Nikolai Pavlovich Shelestun (36 Ostrovsky Street,
Novaya Boyarka, Kiev Region), whose turn it was to receive
us. At 8.30 p.m. a uniformed district lieutenant of the police
arrived with seven men in plain clothes and they broke into
our meeting . . .

Trying to note down all those present, they seized the
identity card of the owner of the house and said, "You'll pay
for this." Then they ordered him to appear at the Boyarka
police station.

He presented himself there at 4.45 p.m. on April 2, 1967,
and after a quarter of an hour he was summoned into the
office of the chief of police, with whom were the prosecutor
and some local officials. When Shelestun, the father of two
children, had been put in a chair away from the table, the
chief of police asked him his name. Then he came up from
behind and said, "You've been a pain to us, now we'll be a
pain to you," and he struck Shelestun's head with his fist.
The prosecutor, who had been sitting by the table, also began
from the other side to beat him on the head, face, back of the
neck and ears. When he asked why he was being beaten like
this, they replied with obscenities and added, "We're going
to tear your guts out and we shan't answer." Then the chief
of police knelt down in front of the man he had beaten up,
joined his hands and mocked, "Now ask God to save you
from us." Shelestun lost consciousness from the blows and
slumped from the chair to the floor.

After this first attack, they pulled him up by the hair on to
the chair again, brought an official form with a blank space
and ordered him to sign. When he refused to do so, they
again began to beat him and yelled at him to sign. On this
form were the words, "At a religious meeting in the house of
N. P. Shelestun anti-Soviet leaflets were read." Because he
refused to sign this false statement, he was again beaten. He

once more fell to the floor unconscious, where the militia continued to kick him. As he was now bleeding profusely, the chief of police ordered him to wipe the blood off and then took away two handkerchiefs saturated with the blood which was flowing from Shelestun's mouth and nose.

At 7 p.m. they threatened to send Shelestun to the police headquarters in Kiev (15 Korolenko Street), but instead they searched his pockets, seized his personal belongings and sent him home with the words, "Warn your friends that the same fate awaits them."

... We inform you that these actions are a continuation of the physical assault and violence being used against people for their religious convictions.

By commission of the 400 members of the Kiev Baptist Church, 78 people signed.
April 5, 1967.
...

*Living conditions of Baptist detainees in camps and prisons*

Baptist believers in the camps have been subjected to especially difficult conditions.

Contrary to the rules laid down for corrective camps, they are deprived of the right to correspond with friends and relatives. Letters in which the word 'God' or other phrases of religious content appear are held back and not permitted ... In the Kaluga camp the authorities burned a packet of unread letters before the eyes of Mikhail Khorev ...

The general position is that Baptist prisoners in the camps are not permitted to have Bibles or Gospels, on the grounds that they are pernicious books ... They are not permitted to fulfil their spiritual obligation of participating in the Lord's Supper. Other democratic countries even provide chaplains for prisons and camps out of state funds, but we are deprived of the right of having even our own ministers for this purpose. What legal basis is there for this? ... The punishment cell threatens many prisoners for saying their prayers. We have data on this from many camps and prisons ...

Vera Petrovna Shuportyak, who is in a Potma camp, was deprived of visits and two months' mail for refusal to work on a Sunday, although prior to this she had been working twelve hours a day. She is exhausted and very weak . . .

Baptists in the camps are terrorized by constant interrogations and threats and they are forbidden to see each other . . .

Alexei Kozorezov contracted heart trouble while languishing in a room without daylight . . . Lidia Govorun is seriously ill at Potma, after being arrested and sentenced as a member of the Council of Prisoners' Relatives and for petitioning for the release of prisoners. Her son, Seryozha, was seized and is now in a boarding school at Smolensk . . .

### Forcible internment of Baptists in mental hospitals

. . . On October 17, 1966, the Baptist V. P. Kolesnik came to the premises of the Central Committee of the Communist Party for a personal interview with Mr. Shelepin. He was seeking the restoration of his pension which had been stopped by order to the secretary of the Sinelnikovo Party Committee (Dnepropetrovsk Region). From the Central Committee reception room he was removed to Moscow Psychiatric Hospital No. 15, where he was interrogated about internal church affairs.

P. Safronov, a believer, was arrested on June 21, 1966, at Ryazan. On September 23 that year he was transferred to the Serpsky Psychiatric Institute in Moscow. We do not know what kind of experiments were carried out on him, nor in what condition we shall find him when we see him again, but we do know that he was in good health when arrested. On January 13, 1967, he was sentenced to six years' imprisonment under Article 70 of the Penal Code of the Russian Republic. [A political article.]

There have been other similar instances . . .

### Confiscation of private homes and prayer-houses

With the aim of liquidating congregations and preventing them from holding religious services, numerous prayer-houses have been confiscated and not returned in very many towns and villages ... Private houses of believers are confiscated if religious worship is held there.

For example, in 1966 at Podolsk (Moscow Region), V. V. Kuznetsova's house was taken away from her because worship had been held there. This is how it happened. While she was out at work, policemen and auxiliaries drove up to the house. They loaded all her possessions into the vehicle, seized the deeds of the house, turned her elderly mother out into the street and posted a guard with a dog outside. In the meantime, the authorities had called Kuznetsova from work and informed her of the sentence that her house was to be confiscated. All petitions for its return were fruitless. As a result, she has become a vagrant, normal living conditions having been denied her ...

*Humiliation of Baptist children for their religious sentiments*

... In July 1966 Leonid Grigorievich Oleinik, a boy of eleven at Shakhty Secondary School No. 1 (who lived at 44 Vasyuta Street) was summoned to appear before Mr. Skakun, a detective from the Prosecutor's Office. He was interrogated about the believers, Andryushina, Popova and Pali. Leonid had been summoned to the Prosecutor's Office together with his elder sister, Lilia, but the detective did not allow her to be present during the interrogation. Skakun and his henchmen even showed Leonid photographs of a man whose hand had been cut off, his eye plucked out and his face mutilated. Then they said, "This is what we do to the likes of you who won't give evidence." After such threats, Leonid was forced to sign a document which had been drawn up by Skakun ...

Nelya Khrenova, a girl of seven at Lutsky School No. 10, was intimidated in December 1966 by her teacher, Nadezhda Trofimovna, when the pupils were being given injections. She said to the nurse, "Give her ten shots because she believes in God". Then she said to Nelya, "Don't come to school if you're going to believe in God". ...

*Children seized*

. . . On March 28, 1967, at Tomsk, Vera Kureibina, a girl
of thirteen, who lived at 32 Karpovsky Lane, was kidnapped
and forcibly put in a children's home. Her parents have even
been prevented from seeing their daughter freely.

A precisely similar offence was committed in the village of
Novaya Titrovka (Dinskaya District, Krasnodar Territory),
where Vitya Slyusarev, a boy of fourteen, was kidnapped on
February 10, 1967. To this day, his parents do not know
where their son is. They have been barred not only from
visiting him, but even from writing to him. . .

*A Prisoner's Testimony (Pavel Overchuk)*

We have omitted many of the examples which substantiate the
main points of the above document with specific instances. We
must, however, because of its intrinsic importance and because
it has not been published elsewhere, quote more fully from the
single example of the prison experiences of Pavel Overchuk.
On May 10, 1967, he wrote a complaint to the prosecutor of the
Ukraine about his treatment in a corrective labour colony near
Kiev. He had been sentenced on September 24, 1966, to two-
and-a-half years for his religious activities when he was thirty-
four years old. He wrote:

In these corrective labour colonies, my fellow-believers and I
have our rights infringed in every possible way for no other
reason than that we are believers. I was with five fellow-
Baptists . . . in Camp No. 65 (Kiev Region) and we submitted a petition to the U.S.S.R. Ministry for the Protection
of Public Order to obtain permission, according to the
statute laid down which regulates the rights of prisoners, to
perform the Christian ceremony of the breaking of bread.
This is an integral part of the Baptist faith and it is obligatory for all church members. Instead of granting our most
minimal religious requirements, the camp administration
section of the Ukrainian branch of the ministry retained our
petition and did not forward it to Moscow. Instead, they
gave an irresponsible answer of their own—irresponsible,

because in their refusal there is no reference to any relevant point of our legislation which denies even minimal satisfaction of the religious needs of believers in corrective labour colonies . . .

On April 19, 1967, I was informed at the commission and in conversation with the camp commandant that I had no right to believe in God and pray to Him. I replied that such statements were unlawful, that I was a believer and could not live a single day without praying to my God, the Creator of the whole universe and of all living things.

The camp administration made various threats. They told me that their people would be attached to me [recruits of the security agencies among the prisoners]. They would observe me and eavesdrop on any word I should say to anyone about God; if I should worship God, I would be severely punished. I declared that it was not necessary to put spies on to me, for I would admit at once that I had prayed to God while at liberty, in prison and in Camp 65; if I had not prayed, I would have been a free man instead of being there.

On April 26, 1967, my mother, an old woman of seventy-one whose husband had died at the front, came to see me with some other relatives.

I took an application for a general visit and food parcel to I. P. Chelnokov, the division commander, who said, however, that no visits could be granted to a person who prays to God. I replied that through no fault of my own I had not had a visit for five months and had not received any food parcels for three months, despite the fact that as a normal-régime prisoner I should have been allowed both a general visit and a food parcel every two months. Nowhere was it mentioned that a believer who prays to God should not have a visit.

The Commandant's reply was that he had consulted with the prosecutor, who had told him that they had the right to deprive me of all privileges, for I was praying to God in the presence of other prisoners in the barracks where I slept. I replied that, under the conditions of my detention, there was nowhere I could pray to God without other prisoners seeing me, but if they were to give me some other more convenient place, I would use it. Again the division commandant forbade me to pray and threatened that, unless I ceased to do so, I would be put in the *shizo* [solitary confinement punishment cell] instead of receiving a visit. If this did not work, they would put me permanently into a prison-régime cellblock, where I would be deprived of any possibility of correspondence and visits and where they would allow me to receive only one food parcel every six months. I would not be allowed to buy supplies in the prison shop and would be forced to do hard physical labour on a reduced food ration. I would have to stay there until the end of my sentence. If even this did not work, they would cut out my liver and would force me to carry out the orders of the camp administration and stop praying to God. I replied that such acts would be illegal, as I had the right to believe in God and confess my faith. Prayer, moreover, was in indispensable part of the Baptist faith.

These legitimate requests were all repeated at a higher level, but Pavel Overchuk received no satisfaction whatsoever. Eventually a senior official, Lieutenant-Colonel Mechkan, told him to "go and pray in the toilet".

I replied that I had not yet lost my human nature, I still had feelings of human dignity and was not going to pray in such a place. Furthermore, such remarks insulted my religious feelings and brought no honour to a senior camp official entrusted with people's education ... Thus, instead of receiving the visit now due to me, they put me in the *shizo* over the Easter and May holidays (April 26 to May 6, 1967).

What is a *shizo* like?

It is a cell without windows, light or air, about twelve to fourteen square yards in area. Electric light filters in through a Judas-window covered by a thick grille about twelve to sixteen inches high and the width of the door (five-and-a-half feet). After they have had their warm clothes, handkerchiefs and bedding taken away, twelve, fifteen or more people are crowded into a cell like this and deprived of air and light. In such a cell you can sleep only in a crouching or sitting position on the floor or on a raised wooden platform.

During the whole ten days the cell is not opened for airing, and the prisoners may not leave it for a single moment, not even to relieve themselves or to attend to minimal hygienic necessities. Food is served through a hatch. One day there is a pound of black bread and a small tin of hot water, the next day a little bit of tasteless, cold food with no fat content (the ration for five days is less than a normal prisoner receives in one).

Naturally, conditions like these encourage parasites to multiply—and this happened in my case. On the eighth day, a great swarm of lice appeared. For two days, the prisoners asked for disinfectants and finally the head of the sanitary department was summoned. He ordered that we should have a bath and the cell be dusted, which was done. But when we returned from the bathroom we saw that the floor of the cell was covered with a layer of insecticide between one and two inches deep. The prisoners asked that the dust should be removed or the cell washed out. Although the prisoners could not avoid inhaling the powder, the request was refused and they were allowed only to sweep the insecticide to the base of the walls.

One may ask whether all this stopped my praying to God. On the contrary, I came to value all the more the divine gifts of fresh air and light. I have been shown how base is the influence of atheism, which is not an ideological struggle with believers, but deliberately sets out to destroy them physically.

I have come to believe all the more in the pre-eminence of Christ and His Gospel, which is light and enlightens every man, influencing his spirit, awakening his mind and conscience, raising him from his lowly corrupt and sinful condition to a loftier spiritual height. Through atheistic education and the *shizo*, however, man is merely coarsened, because he lives in conditions worse than those a good master would provide for his animals . . .

*Vins in the Labour Camp*

Horrifying as they are, Pavel Overchuk's prison experiences are remarkable for the detail in which he describes them (and for the fact that the document was somehow smuggled out of the prison) rather than for any particular brutality which was perpetrated on him. At the same time, his spiritual leader, Georgi Vins, was undergoing experiences which were very similar to the sufferings of prisoners in concentration camps during the height of Stalinism. Not content with the humiliations which had been heaped upon him during his trial, the authorities now considered it necessary to inflict on him working conditions which could well have caused his death.

We have no comparable record of the treatment of Gennadi Kryuchkov in his camp in the Chita Region in Siberia, just north of Outer Mongolia. Vins, having been sent to Kizel in the Ural Mountains, was perhaps slightly more accessible. Either one of his relatives or friends managed to visit him and report back to his congregation at Kiev about his physical condition, or Vins himself succeeded in sending such information out of the camp.

On February 25, 1968, less than half-way through his sentence, 176 Baptists from Kiev signed a petition to Mr. Brezhnev, to the head of the KGB and to many other official Soviet bodies and newspapers. The stark details make this one of the most terrifying documents ever to have been sent out of the Soviet Union by a religious community. We shorten it, so as to avoid repetition of the biography already recounted.

. . . No sooner was Vins elected to his office (as a leader of the reform Baptists) than he became subjected to various forms of persecution—slanderous fabrications and baiting in the press, insults, threats of arrest, summonses to the Prosecutor's Office, and so on. Not only he was affected, but his family also. His wife was dismissed from work with a compromising statement in her service record, so that up to now she has been unable to enjoy the constitutional right to work;[4] his daughter has been terrorized at school . . .

In February 1967, Vins was sent to serve his sentence in

one of the camps in the Perm Region and in the summer of the same year he was transferred to another camp. His address is P.O.B. 201–10 'A', Taly Postal District, Kizel.

The conditions under which he is being held in this camp reveal both the true reasons for his transfer and the real motives of the authorities.

The Kiev Baptist congregation possesses reliable information about the invention of certain bodies to liquidate Georgi Petrovich Vins through his camp conditions. Because all this has been implemented, he is now physically right at the end of his tether. In violation of the relevant regulations of the Ministry for the Protection of Public Order, which govern the treatment of prisoners in camps, Vins, when he arrived at the camp, was forced to join a building brigade and had to march to work under guard five or six miles in each direction every day (ten or twelve miles in all) through rugged, mountainous terrain. Although by profession a qualified engineer, he was used as a beast of burden, hauling logs manually from the forest to construct a railway.

In these camp conditions, Vins contracted an infection in October 1967, from which his body has not yet recovered and which, combined with the physical slavery, has worn him out completely and given him heart trouble. In addition, permanent running sores have appeared all over his arms and body. On occasions he has lost consciousness on his way to work or while on the job, but despite his physical condition he has not been exempted from work. Finally, because the work was beyond his strength, he contracted a double inguinal hernia. Yet even after this he was still forced to do this hard physical labour, although this meant that his health would be irreparably broken and even his life would be endangered. . .

Because of the continuous threats of officialdom to liquidate Vins and because they are obviously already well on the way to being carried out, we believers, as well as Vins himself and his relatives, distrust any surgical intervention which might be carried out on camp premises—and we have every reason to hold this view.

At the same time, the camp administration, despite its

need for electricians and repeated requests from Vins himself, his relatives and the Council of Baptist Prisoners' Relatives, refuses to employ him in his profession of electrical engineer and continues to make him do physical labour.

Moreover, on January 26, 1968, Major Tesov, deputy commandant of the Taly prison complex, instructed the camp commander, in the presence of Vins himself, to employ him, a sick man, on especially heavy physical labour!
This decisively demonstrates the intention of the said authorities to take advantage of Vins's term of sentence for his physical liquidation.

Apart from all this, Vins was subjected to other forms of illegal deprivation. They confiscated the Bible which he had had during his time in prison. The Procurator's Office and other bodies have created such an atmosphere in the camp that he has been forced to forgo all visits from his relatives and children, for even these were being exploited to terrorize him through threats, suspicions which were being cast on him and deterioration of his situation. Moreover, parcels sent to him by post and due to him once a month, according to the existing regulations, are frequently returned, as a result of the deliberately callous attitude of the camp authorities.

According to existing regulations, Vins should be released before the end of his sentence, as he has never infringed camp rules. The camp administration recommended him for early release, but the Taly commission refused to grant this. Here we have evidence of discrimination against Vins because of his religious convictions and, in the light of all the above, our fears for his life have been increased.

We, the Baptists of Kiev, are deeply shocked at the attempts being made to liquidate our brother, G. P. Vins, the more so because the fate which befell our fellow-believers Khmara, Vibe and others, in the camps is still fresh in our minds. Only recently we learned that Lanbin, a believer from Novosibirsk, has been allowed to die in a camp.

The Kiev Baptists ended their appeal by making three specific requests to the authorities: that Vins should be given lighter work, that an investigation commission should be set up to look into his treatment in the camps, and that the cases of all those imprisoned for religious reasons should be reviewed, with the aim that they should be rehabilitated.

Despite the appalling conditions to which he had been subjected, Vins still did not lose his will to live. His faith sustained him, despite being deprived of his Bible. We have proof of this, because he even managed to write some poetry in his labour camp. We have one short poem which he somehow managed to send out. It reached Aida Skripnikova and we have a transcription of it in her own handwriting, dated June 9, 1967 (it is not clear whether this was the day on which the poem was written or upon which Aida copied it). At any rate, Aida managed to send it out of the country before she was herself arrested the next year. Here is the whole poem, addressed to Pastor Makhovitsky, who was with Vins in prison and whom he calls his 'brother':

> Tears held back in the eyes of friends—
> Often, often glisten . . .
> No! They have not been caused
> By the yoke of camps in the *taiga*.
>
> Deportations and sad dungeons
> Cannot cause the grief of friends,
> But only those dearest faces
> Of children abandoned far away.
>
> Remembering their childish talk,
> My dear brother suddenly fell sad—
> A letter had come from his own home
> And children's photographs!
>
> Those dearest faces call you home,
> Love burns in their eyes . . .
> A tear of crystal purity
> Trembled then upon your eye!
>
> The Lord gives His salvation,
> Offering love without restraint—
> Lord, hear a father's prayer
> For his dearest little children!

Stretch forth your powerful right hand
And soften the wrath of men,
Open for us this hard prison
And give these children back their father!

Utterly simple in its language and emotion though it is, this poem cannot be rendered in English with the true flavour of the original, which is reminiscent of the finest classical Russian poetry in its purity.

Despite the dreadful physical ordeal, despite the persistent circulation of rumours in the West that Georgi Vins was dead, the wish of his poem was fulfilled. Makhovitsky was released at the end of 1968, his sentence completed. Kryuchkov was released in 1969, and immediately resumed active leadership of the Reform Movement.

According to one report, Vins was accused of supporting the people of Czechoslovakia near the end of his sentence, but he reacted to the threats by going on a twenty-day hunger strike. Following his release his wife and friends took him away to a quiet hospital. After an operation for hernia, he was given a spell of rest and was then ready to return to active service as a pastor and to continue his fight for justice.

Vladimir Kuroyedov, head of the government Council for Religious Affairs, rounded on the 'liars' in the West who had circulated rumours of the death of Vins and Bondarenko, saying that they were people who were out to misrepresent the religious situation in the Soviet Union in order to further their anti-communist crusade (*Izvestia*, October 18, 1969). Kuroyedov omitted to explain how these young, healthy men became so seriously ill during their prison sentences.

## The Reformers Fight On

Arrests and intimidation had continued throughout the years that Vins and Kryuchkov remained in prison. Sentences in some instances became even harsher. So it was with Trofim Feidak and Vladimir Vilchinsky, resolute leaders of the Brest Baptists, whose registration had been taken away from them in 1960. Eight years of unremitting struggle to regain their lost legal status, a struggle which had naturally brought them to support Kryuchkov and Vins, resulted in a conviction to five years' imprisonment each on April 17, 1968. The sentence, which is above the maximum of three years under the laws controlling religious activity, is explained by the fact that they were found guilty under two separate clauses and the sentences were not permitted to run concurrently. We have extensive legal records of their trial.

A feature of some of these new court cases was the extreme youth of the defendants. Raisa Burmai was arrested in the Ukraine in 1968, when she was a mere seventeen, but she does not seem to have remained in prison for long. Much less fortunate was Yevgeni Rodoslavov, from Odessa. He was only eighteen when arrested, according to the testimony of a letter signed by 180 other young Baptists from his home town. It seems that he had done no more than take a leading part in the organization of local Baptist youth work. His trial took place in that atmosphere of hysteria which we have already come to know so well. Two days before it opened, a local paper pronounced him guilty. Defence witnesses were treated as if they themselves had been accused of dastardly crimes. Young sympathizers standing outside the court were beaten up without any intervention from the police. Rodoslavov was given a sentence of almost incredible severity (even by Soviet standards)—five years in a prison camp, followed by five years of exile. This was the same as Prokofiev, the instigator of the movement, had been given. Finally, there was a campaign to terrorize all the other Baptists of the area. In a public lecture a school headmaster increased the hysteria by accusing local Baptists of crucifying a girl in an act of ritual murder.

The news recently filtering through about prison-camp conditions gives no ground for increased optimism. Indeed, a report has come from Tula, where people who had been in touch with Ivan Afonin have found out that he died at the Komsomolsky camp in that region on November 22, 1969. He had apparently been forced to work when seriously ill, as Georgi Vins had been. He had been doing a three-year sentence since March 1967. He was forty-three.

A new development, and a very impressive one, has been the

founding of another organization associated with the Council of Churches. A 'Union of Christian Baptist Mothers' is now in existence. We do not know exactly when it was founded, but in 1969 it acted decisively. It is very similar to, but not the same as, the Council of Prisoners' Relatives. Its terms of reference are to gather all the information it can about the maltreatment of children because of their religious faith. So, although mothers of some children whose fathers had been imprisoned might belong to it, it is open to others as well.

In March 1969 the Union sent an appeal to Brezhnez and no less than twenty-four other government officials, agencies and newspapers. Its ten closely written pages confirm much of and add vivid detail to what has been set out in our narrative, but the most impressive feature of the document is its voluminous appendix. This consists of forty pages of lists of signatures—no less than 1,453 of them, from forty-two different towns and villages distributed widely over seven republics, including places as far apart as Barnaul in Siberia and the same Brest (on the Polish frontier) which we have just mentioned. The Ukraine is particularly strongly represented. The document in the West has the original signatures, not typed copies of them, and a number of these names were already known for their Christian activities.

Of the various types of protest movement now germinating in the U.S.S.R., only the Crimean Tartars, who were deported *en masse* by Stalin and are now trying to win the right to return to their homeland, have ever collected more signatures under a single document. Even they did not come from such a wide variety of geographical locations.

This new movement demonstrates not only the resilience of these women in the face of nine years' unremitting persecution (not to mention earlier tribulations), but also a degree of co-ordination and organization which is unique for an unrecognized (and therefore illegal) body trying to maintain contacts among its members under such adverse conditions.

The Baptist Mothers give evidence of the further deterioration of the situation in 1968. They say that there were sixty-four more arrests among their fellow-believers, as a result of which about two hundred additional children are suffering, either because they have been deprived of the family bread-winner or because they have been forcibly moved into boarding schools. Some of the youngest of them are being thrown into prison with their parents and the writers are extremely concerned about the psychological damage this might cause.

You are flinging their pure hearts, as yet untainted by vice, into a society of criminals, into a circle of people whose morals have completely disintegrated. For several years on end they are to be witnesses of such depravity as you would never allow your own children to see. The deep spiritual wounds which they receive there in the camps can never be effaced. Their tears are being collected by God and will weigh on your consciences like a heavy millstone of ineradicable guilt.

The compilation includes several contributions signed by individuals and recounting specific cases. One of these is by Nadezhda Sloboda, then aged thirty-three, and her husband, from the village of Dubravy, Belorussia. On February 11, 1966, they were sentenced to loss of parental rights and their two daughters, Galya, aged eleven, and Shura, aged nine, were removed to a boarding-school, because their parents had been bringing them up as Christians. This is how the parents described what ensued:

Living for two years in a children's home, in insanitary conditions, the children were shaved because of lice, Galya's feet suppurated from constantly damp foot-wear and twice they were ill with scabies. They were deprived of letters from their parents and finally the children decided to risk their lives and escape back home. So at 9 p.m. on January 4 this year (1968) they arrived frozen at their house.

The police came after three days. There was a row, but they allowed the children to remain for the time being. Then a month later the police came to the village school:

The headmaster told Galya that she had to return to the

children's home, at which point the policeman, Lebed, came
out from behind a cupboard and instantly fell upon her. He
carried her to the car. She was shouting, "Help! Help!" and
trying with all her might to wrench herself free. The policeman fell in the struggle, but did not release his prey from his
arms.

Shura was taken, too, and then the car moved off with the
children screaming.

The compilers of the document add a sequel to this. Nadezhda Sloboda was sentenced on December 11, 1968, to a
prison term of four years. The children were allowed home for
their winter holiday soon after, but found no mother waiting to
greet them. There is even a letter from the children themselves.

On October 1, 1968, a new law on marriage and the family
came into effect in the Soviet Union which denies parents the
right to bring up children according to their own religious
beliefs. They must 'rear their children in the spirit of the moral
code of the builder of communism'; 'exerting a harmful
influence' on them can result in a court case and deprivation of
parental rights (Articles 18 and 19). Although such deprivation
had in fact been occuring previously, the Mothers' document
gives evidence that it had been much easier to carry out since
the passing of the new law.

Even where parents are not being imprisoned or their
children removed, unpleasant situations can arise, particularly
where schoolteachers incite their pupils against other children
who are Christians. An especially frightening example of this is
quoted by N. Rudich. It concerns a village schol at Bobrovitsa,
in the Ukraine. From September 1968 her son, Volodya, was
forced by his teacher, Miss Cherednichenko, to wear a red star
badge. When he repeatedly refused, she began systematically to
stand him in the corner every day. His mother goes on:

His class-mates, urged on by their teacher, similarly made
him stand in the corner before lessons began. The teacher
nicknamed him 'Little Jesus' and reduced his conduct marks
by four, which made the children hostile towards my son ...

As a result, his class-mates, V. Menshun, A. Ovodov and V. Shestun, did something terrible. On November 19, 1968, on the way home from school, they threw my son Voldya on the roadway underneath a moving tractor. Only thanks to the quick reaction of the driver, who braked sharply, was my son not killed.

Even after this, the other children beat him up severely, but the doctors tried to conceal the whole episode by diagnosing a 'bad cold and catarrh' and consigning him to psychological tests.

The whole tenor of the document suggests that in their present mood nothing short of arrest is likely to restrain these 1,453 women from continuing their fight for justice—and that to remove them would persuade yet more to champion their cause. Here is the dilemma which confronts the Soviet atheists at the present stage of their policy (if indeed they can be said to have any rational policy at all). Direct repression has failed to have the desired effect and the circle of protest has been persistently widening. But if the authorities ease off in their campaign, this might give these brave Christians the chance to establish Sunday schools, to broaden their influence still more and to deepen their solidarity by increasing contacts with fellow-believers from other countries.

At the same time as new arrests have been made, other Baptists besides Georgi Vins and Gennadi Kryuchkov were released at the end of their sentences. By the end of 1969, according to one report, no less than eighty had been released, including most of the leaders who had been imprisoned in 1966. Nevertheless, it is a highly precarious liberty. Dedicated and uncompromising men, such as Iosif Bondarenko (who had what Kuroyedov described as a 'noisy wedding' soon after his release) must know that a resumption of their evangelical activities will inevitably lead to another imprisonment.

At least for a short time, the best men in the movement were free to negotiate with the leaders of the All-Union Council for a reconciliation.

*Towards Reconciliation?*

As soon as they were free and fit again, the reform leaders gave these negotiations a high priority. They wanted to resolve in a brotherly spirit the issues which still separated the two bodies. Activity on these lines had continued in some form from the time of the congress of October 1966, though it obviously could not be representative on the side of the Council of Churches, since all their top leaders were in prison.

The All-Union Council did, however, set up a unity commission and there is every evidence that it took its task of finding an ultimate solution very seriously. Certainly some people who had formerly been associated with the reformers were appointed to it and played an active role. The commission seems to have taken great care to treat the reform movement with consideration—with too much consideration, some said. At the 1969 official All-Union Congress, Pastor V. I. Lebedev, its secretary, a former supporter of the reformers, said (according to the *Fraternal Messenger*, no. 2, 1969, p. 64) that some people had incorrectly accused the commission of supporting the reformers' position. There were, he claimed, some members of it who wrongly insisted on treating it as a 'neutral organization', and not as an arm of the AUCECB. It looks, in other words, as though there were people on the commission who regarded it as their responsibility to penetrate into the heart of the rights and wrongs of the situation, in an impartial attempt to find a solution. Lebedev's strictures on this attitude fill one with misgivings about what the commission could hope to achieve when it was acting as an instrument for enforcing decisions in favour of one side only. It was further claimed at the 1969 congress by Alexander Karev that about 3,600 'schismatics' had rejoined the Union since the previous congress three years earlier—not a particularly impressive figure, even if completely accurate (and one has long since learned to treat with extreme caution all statistics to do with religion in the Soviet Union).

Meetings between the All-Union Council and the reformers took place on April 19 and May 17, 1969. Five took part from the reformers' side and seven from the official body, including

Shaptala, Pavlov, Golev, Khorev and Vinogradsky, of whom
the last three had only recently been released from prison after
serving their full sentences. This is the first such occasion of
which we have a reasonably full and frank account from both
sides. Sergei Golev, one of the most revered leaders of the
reform movement, was negotiating under severe duress, it later
transpired. Once again he had come under investigation on
April 3, 1969 (we have the full legal findings). He may well
have been threatened to find a solution—'or else!' He certainly
had reason to fear, assuming he knew a case had already been
taken up against him—and it would be consistent with Soviet
methods if such threats were used. It seems that relations between the two sides were very friendly at the first session in
April, but the second meeting a month later failed to fulfil this
promise. The All-Union Council stated on May 26 that in the
prayers and hymn-singing at the outset there was felt a keen
desire that the Lord should give them 'unity and love and
inspire them with gentleness, humility and mutual forgiveness'.
This is confirmed by the reformers.

According to the All-Union Council, they proposed at the
first meeting that the reformers should accept the modified
Baptist programme as put forward at the congresses of 1963
and 1966, together with admissions of former errors which
were made on both occasions. There would then be a basis
for discussions and the eventual achievement of unity in all
local congregations.

The reformers report that on their side they brought forward
a number of questions which were discussed. First of all, they
wanted a much clearer explanation than they had ever received
of precisely why the *New Statutes* and *Letters of Instructions*
had ever been adopted in the first place; they wanted a resolution of conflicting explanations which had been put forward.
Some of the All-Union delegates admitted that this had been a
sinful act which had subsequently been corrected; one maintained that the actions were justified at the time they were
adopted; others argued that they were not the sole cause of the
schism in any case.

Secondly, the reformers wanted a strong assurance from the
All-Union Council, that what Prokofiev, Kryuchkov and Vins

had done was no longer regarded as 'the fire of the devil' (the expression which they said that Alexander Karev once used). Apparently, the All-Union Council claimed that this had never been more than an individual opinion, but the reformers referred to an official letter from the Council of June 20, 1962, in which the new movement was called 'an enemy of our holy work'.

Thirdly, the reformers asked whether the All-Union Council looked on the prisoners as true servants of God, or as people who had been sentenced for their unwise conduct. The reformers pointed out that by consistently representing them as people who encouraged their followers to break the law the All-Union Council had played no small part in incensing the State authorities against them. To represent the whole conflict as being basically about attitudes to the law was not completely true. After all, calling for a representative congress was not the same as inciting people to break the law; and in any case the relevant law had been passed in 1929 and all parties had lived under it without serious schism until 1960, so it was the events of that year which must be reviewed to explain the dispute.

Fourthly, the reformers were deeply disturbed by the reports of what was being said about them by the All-Union Council at international Christian gatherings. In particular, they requested to see a document presented to the executive committee of the Baptist World Alliance at its meeting in Africa, July 28–31, 1968. The reformers emphasized that they were expecting no help from outside except prayers, but such prayers should be founded only upon objective knowledge of the situation.

The All-Union Council and the reformers, despite some continuing disagreements, seemed to get on well personally and to establish a very definite common base from which to set out on the quest for future unity.

Unfortunately, these relations seem to have been soured in the interval between the two meetings. The All-Union Council lays the blame on the reformers for breaking an alleged agreement of silence on the content of the discussions at the first meeting, and communicating what had occurred in their *Fraternal Leaflet* No. 5 of 1969. They quote a passage from this publication warning against embarking upon any local discussions on unity for the time being.

In reply to this charge, the reformers say that they did no more than inform congregations that the April session had taken place and try to counter certain local representatives of the All-Union Council, who were initiating discussions in their own churches based upon false information which they were supplying.

At the May session the atmosphere certainly deteriorated. The reformers, in their account, say they were seriously disturbed because the All-Union Council had withdrawn its offer to make an open act of repentance for having put forward the disputed documents of 1960. They seemed now to regard such repentance as 'unpatriotic'. Further, the All-Union Council did not fulfil the promise it had allegedly given to make available the document presented to the Executive Committee of the Baptist World Alliance. Also, the All-Union Council had now reverted to the old habit of calling the reformers 'schismatics'.

It is not clear whether there was any other reason for the deterioration of the relationship between the two meetings beyond the alleged broken agreement by the reformers about the secrecy of the first meeting. One wonders whether any state pressure had been brought to bear on the All-Union Council on the 'repentance' issue. If Church leaders were to apologize publicly for yielding to outside influences, this would obviously be a sensitive point for the authorities themselves and they might fear it would weaken their position in future dealings with the Church. It is also more than possible that information about the new charge against Sergei Golev which was pending (allegedly for his publishing activities) had circulated between this meeting and the one held the previous month.

With this, as with so much else in the life of the Russian Churches, the real truth remains hidden from us and we are left once again in the realm of speculation. What is certain is that after the second meeting the two sides parted in an atmosphere considerably less cordial than after the first. The reformers regretted that hopes which had been raised a month earlier had been dashed, and they referred to the continuing 'false pride' of the All-Union Council members. The latter seemed less pessimistic and gave the text of an agreement which they were prepared to sign, but which the reformers said they must show to their fellow Christians before they could say 'yes' or 'no' to it. The main points in it were these:

1. Judgment on any guilt incurred through adopting the 1960 documents on the one side and through sharp accusations on the other should be left to God himself. Holy Scripture alone should decide the question of the excommunications which had been pronounced on both sides (the first time, incidentally, that there has been any admission from the All-Union Council that it had itself denied fellowship to people in the local churches who supported the reform).
2. Mutual recriminations must cease.
3. Forgiving one another in Christ offered the hope that there would be a way forward through the many difficulties ahead.
4. Meetings together must continue.
5. This agreement must be published for the whole Church to see.

Two months after his second meeting Sergei Golev, who had already spent nineteen of his seventy-three years in prison on various falsified charges, was arrested at Ryazan. Ten days later the investigation was concluded (showing that the essential part of it had been carried out before the arrest). On September 10 he was tried and given three years in a strict-régime camp. It is a testimony to his character that it was found necessary, at his age, by the passing of such a severe sentence, to add to the sufferings of a man who had already undergone so much.

Despite the arrest of Golev, attempts at a reconciliation continued. I. G. Ivanov, the President of the All-Union Council, wrote to Vins in June, inviting him to take part in the discussions. Vins insisted that the request should be sent formally to all the elected leaders of the Council of Churches. On October 9, 1969, such a letter was received and further consultation between the two sides took place on October 29 and December 4.

The talks apparently stuck again over the issue of 'repentance'. The representatives of the All-Union Council showed some willingness to express repentance for having adopted the *New Statutes* in 1960, but they would do it only if the reformers would offer penitence from their side also. This they resolutely refused to do, obviously feeling that their prison sentences had justified the rightness of what they had done. The All-Union Council put forward a new document, but the reformers found it completely unacceptable. In *Fraternal Leaflet* No. 2, 1970, the reformers quoted a letter they had written to the All-Union Council on February 25:

> You declined our proposition [of repenting] and began to circulate the draft you had drawn up, falsely making it out to be a 'Joint Declaration'. It did not even have a date and you received no reply to it from the Council of Churches. Yet later you put a date on it yourselves and circulated it as a document reflecting a two-sided agreement ... As you certainly know that there had been no agreement between us on the question of unity, you have deluded quite a number of ECB congregations.
>
> By these actions you have once again demonstrated that not only are you making no hint of repentance for the past, but you are even committing new acts which are so essentially sinful as to be almost in the same category as the *Statutes* and *Letter of Instructions* of 1960.

The letter ended by saying that certainly not all of the All-Union Council representatives were to blame for what had happened, but it was a pity that they had maintained silence.

## Further Conferences

In November 1969 the resilient Council of Prisoners' Relatives for the first time organized an All-Union congress and met at an unidentified place. No minutes of their sessions are available (at the time of writing), but we do have the list of 176 prisoners which they compiled. This list confirmed that several reformers had been released during the year and the total number then in prison fell below the two-hundred mark for the first time in several years. However, as the participants pointed out, recent trends were not optimistic and a number of new names had been added during the year. This list for the time included the nationality of many of the prisoners and again gave the detailed addresses of nearly a hundred prison camps.

This congress issued an appeal 'To all Christian Churches; to all Christians of the World', which gave some general reflections on the past century of Russian Baptist history. Its calm and reasoned tone, with a factual account of sufferings past and present, makes a strong contrast to Kuroyedov's article slandering the reformers which had been printed by *Izvestia* very shortly before the congress convened. The sixty-two signatories of this appeal repudiated his inflammatory accusations with immense restraint and dignity.

In Decemember 1969 there were two further events of significance: a conference held by the reformers on December 6 at Tula and a triennal All-Union congress in Moscow from December 9–11.

The first of these was a unique occasion. It was the first time ever that the State authorities had given permission for the reformers to meet officially. Even though the permission was granted only three days before the conference opened, 120 delegates assembled, representing forty-seven different areas of the Soviet Union.

Gennadi Kryuchkov opened the proceedings and was elected chairman of the meeting. He reported on the activity of the Council of Churches since 1966 (the time when he and the other leaders were imprisoned. He said that some of them had been invited to attend the imminent All-Union congress in Moscow, but the meeting decided unanimously that this should be declined, since they were expressly forbidden the right to speak and vote.

Representatives of six registered congregations attended the meeting, which went on at its evening session to discuss the whole issue of registration. It was decided to issue a call to all congregations that they should apply or reapply for registration, using a new form of application which was now in operation.

Six old candidates and two new ones were put up for election to the Council of Churches, including Kryuchkov and Vins, and they all received the unanimous support of those present. It was further moved that the three members of the former council who were at that moment in prison (I. Ya. Antonov and D. V. Minyakov, as well as Golev) should also be considered as still in office. This, too, was unanimously resolved.

Obviously those present at this meeting must have had high hopes that at last the attitude of the authorities was going to change towards them. If they could now start to register their congregations, which up to now the State had consistently refused, they would feel that the discrimination against them was lessening and they might be able to look forward to a more normal religious life in the future. They probably felt, too, that with such a turn of events it would be easier to negotiate with the All-Union Council over the question of unity.

In a mood of some buoyancy, therefore, they penned a letter to Mr. Kosygin requesting permission for all eight legally-elected members of the Council of Churches to be relieved from the obligation to do secular work (to which, of course, registered pastors under the All-Union Council had always been entitled).

This new mood of confidence was to be short-lived. Many congregations under the Council of Churches had long been seeking registration, but nevertheless renewed their efforts as a result of the new directive from the meeting. Believers at Krivoi Rog reported that they had put in an application on January 4, 1970, but the local police reacted by coming and breaking up their meeting by use of force. Several of them were heavily fined for having met for worship.

Much more serious was a whole new wave of arrests in various parts of the Soviet Union (obviously representing a concerted policy), affecting some of the top leaders of the Council of Churches.

Georgi Vins, having been free for only a few months, was arrested yet again, according to a document signed by his mother and four other members of the Council of Prisoners' Relatives (the actual signatures are on one copy circulating in the West). On January 21, 1970, he was sentenced to a year's forced labour for not being gainfully employed—a direct rebuff of his request to serve full-time as a pastor. A member of the All-Union Council later reported to his foreign contacts that Vins was being allowed to live at home in Kiev while he was serving this sentence, which did not entail removal to a prison, but a new list of Baptist prisoners, dated October 15, 1970, states that he is now 'under investigation' once again.

On January 16, 1970, another top leader of the Council of Churches, Peter Rumachik, was arrested at Dedovsk, near Moscow. He had already served two sentences. Now his father-in-law and brother-in-law were arrested, too, leaving the whole family of thirteen without any of its breadwinners.

Mikhail Khorev, who had taken a prominent part in the Tula consultation in December and who had been at liberty for less than a year after his previous sentence, was arrested at Kishin-yov less than two weeks after the meeting, He was now partially blind. His wife was taken seriously ill at the same time and had to go into hospital, leaving three children of under eight at home unattended. At least ten other Baptists are known to have been arrested at around the same time.

The question arises of what was the purpose of the authorities in allowing the Tula consultation, if it was to be immediately followed by a new wave of repressions. The answer seems to be that the release of most of the leaders in 1969 confronted the authorities with a new problem: the threat of renewed activity among the reformers, which might result in a new wave of uncontrolled evangelism up and down the country. The most likely explanation of the events is that the authorities wanted to isolate the most active leaders of the continuing movement by allowing them to convene—this would also provide the opportunity of discovering their latest attitudes over a number of questions. If the authorities had been hoping the representatives at the consultation would make a call for the reform of Soviet law, and thus lay themselves open to attack, they were disappointed, but the State stepped in nevertheless.

The triennial congress of the All-Union Council from December 9–11 was a different affair altogether. It was a big public, indeed international, occasion, with several foreign guests who took a prominent part. Dr. Ronald Goulding, of the

Baptist World Alliance, was one of them and upon his return he wrote in the *Baptist Times* (London, December 25, 1969) that an overwhelming desire for reunion had been displayed by the delegates and that this had become the dominant theme of the congress. The long summary of the proceedings as printed in the *Fraternal Messenger* (No. 2, 1970) bears this out.

There were 475 delegates and 269 guests present, representing sixty-three regional bodies. Alexander Karev reported at great length and in a tone of optimism about the advances which had been made in a whole range of areas since the last congress three years ago: the theological correspondence course, the printing of the Bible and hymn book, growth in membership (by at least 13,000 in the last three years, excluding the return of 3,600 'schismatics', as he called them, and 2,250 Pentecostals who have joined the Union).

Apart from the urgent task of re-uniting with all the reformers, Karev singled out the question of who has the right to become a pastor or a deacon—an issue which had been the cause of some dissension in the congregations. It was decided that if a man's family were known to be evil-livers, he should not be elected, but if they were morally good people, although atheists, this should be no bar to his election. There are, he said, too many old, illiterate and incompetent pastors. Well-educated young people—who do exist in the congregations—must be encouraged to play an active role in the ministry. This was a top priority.

Although some criticism of the All-Union Council was expressed (particularly for spending too much time on foreign visits and not enough on domestic ones), the general tone—at least as reported in the Council's own organ—was one of satisfaction. Rather bitter criticism of the reformers was expressed by some (particularly by D. D. Shapovalov, senior presbyter of the Kharkov Region). S. T. Timchenko, vice-president of the All-Union Council, gave the main speech on unity. While suggesting that the activities of some of the 'schismatics' were a reproach to the brotherhood, he affirmed that the promulgation of the *Letter of Instructions* and the *New Statutes* in 1960 had been a mistake. This had certainly not been done as a deliberate act of malice and the situation had since been rectified.

Pastor Timchenko sharply repudiated the action of the Council of Prisoners' Relatives after their November congress in allegedly spreading false information to organizations outside the Soviet Union, containing 'rumours about persecution of the church and about the alleged physical liquidation of believers'. (One should perhaps note at this point that not even Ilya Brazhnik,[5] arm of the atheist authorities, questioned the veracity of the facts hitherto contained in the reformers' documents. He seems to have had no answer to the extreme care with which they have been compiled.) Pastor Timchenko went on to criticize those abroad who were allegedly exploiting this information to the detriment of the Soviet Union—in particular, Pastor Richard Wurmbrand and the Ukrainian Baptists in the U.S.A.

Pastor Timchenko ended by paying tribute to the personal conduct of the leaders of the reform movement, including Kryuchkov and Vins, at the unity meetings in October and December.

A succession of lesser-known figures came forward to speak to the theme of unity. The emotional temperature of the congress was heightened by those who said that they were returning from the reformers to the All-Union Council. G. I. Maiboroda made a particular impression, as he had been one of the two spokesmen for the reformers at the 1966 congress. He had undergone a spiritual crisis at the beginning of 1969, but this ended when Pastor Mitskevich visited him and persuaded him to return. He had been greeted by great warmth wherever he had gone subsequently amongst the brethren.

Brother Rak, from Ussuriisk in Siberia, reduced many to tears when he said that he had come almost ten thousand kilometres to beg forgiveness for having criticized the leadership of the All-Union Council.

On the third day of the congress, elections were held and the positions of the top leaders, such as Brothers Ivanov and Karev, were confirmed, with the exception that Pastor Ilya Orlov was dropped as a candidate member of the Council.

As in 1966, there must have been tensions beneath the surface of the congress which of course could not be reported by the *Fraternal Messenger*. The arrest of Sergei Golev, one of the chief negotiators of the reformers, cannot have helped. Other arrests followed, but this time the most incendiary actions of the State—the arrests of Vins, Rumachik and Khorev—followed immediately after the congress.

As far as future negotiations between the two factions are concerned, the conclusion can be only that the State, once again, has made it well nigh impossible for a solution to be sought in an atmosphere of calm which is essential to the pursuance of such delicate discussions.

To the impartial outside observer there seems to be a simple solution: for the State to stop interfering in internal Church affairs and to allow discussion of such issues as legislation on religion. However, the Soviet régime seems as little inclined to allow this in the sixth as in the previous five decades of its history. The difference now, however, is that there are well-educated young people in several religious denominations who are prepared to press the issue. They cannot expect to find it other than crucially difficult, but the indications are that they are unlikely to give in.

## NOTES

1. cf. Appendix p. 183.
2. See a report of their imminent trial in the Soviet newspaper, *Pravda Vostoka*, October 22, 1966.
3. She, like so many other amputees in the U.S.S.R., obviously had no artificial limbs.
4. According to another source, she was able to obtain a menial job, but with no chance of using her specialist knowledge (see p. 132).
5. See pp. 182–9.

## Chapter VII

## PERSPECTIVES

### The Schism and the State

How far should a Christian be prepared to go in accommodating himself to the accepted values of the society in which he lives? This is a question which is probably asked by most Christians from time to time, though there is plenty of evidence that not enough of us ask it often or searchingly enough. One should pause for serious thought before rushing to condemn the All-Union Council for being prepared to allow the Soviet State to dictate terms in its relations with the Church.

In the Soviet Union, of course, the question about compromise is asked in a form which is particularly acute, owing to the official philosophy of State atheism. How far, then, can a Christian accept State legislation which aims at furthering atheism and how far can he yield to those even more insidious pressures which build up below the surface, before he comes out in the open with his opposition?

The reformers gave their answer. They drew a line in 1960. They could accept the *status quo* which had existed for sixteen years before then, but they could not accept the subterranean pressures exerted against the Church in 1960 by the Khrushchev régime, which resulted in the documents which the All-Union Council adopted in that year. (In passing, we should note that a number of influential Russian Orthodox churchmen were equally critical when the parochial structure of their Church altered gravely for the worse in 1961, but they avoided going into schism.)

The schism among the Russian Baptists has forced great issues out into the open, issues of truth, freedom and justice. Precisely because of the importance of what is involved, however, there is a great danger that observers not directly involved in the situation might view the conflict exclusively in black and white terms. It does indeed seem that some people involved in these events have played a saintly role, while others have acted from lower motives. It is easy to portray the reformers as a 'persecuted Church' who have preserved the integrity of the faith in the catacombs, but are being betrayed by fellow-Christians who love the glory and honour of an accepted position and the freedom to travel abroad. The truth is far from being so simple.

First, the whole basis of the activities of the reformers is that direct and open approaches must be made, whether to the All-Union Council, the Soviet Government or world public opinion. Soviet policy has rendered them illegal, but one of their chief aims has been to legalize their position.

Secondly, because of the unpredictability of Soviet policy on registration, the dividing line between technically legal and illegal groups of Baptists remains blurred.

Thirdly, Soviet Baptists, like the rest of us, are human beings. Therefore they all have mixed motives and complicated psychology. The numbers in the glistening white or jet black categories are probably relatively small; there are shades of grey in the camp of the reformers as well as that of the All-Union Council.

The moral blame for the schism rests squarely with the Soviet State. The vast majority of Soviet Baptists want to practise their religious observances and bring up their children quietly and without interference. Had they been allowed to do so, the question of a schism would never have arisen. Nevertheless, the evidence is decisive that it is the All-Union Council and its supporters who have gained the greatest benefit from the reformers' actions.

First, they won some measure of reform of the statutes, which everyone now agrees was beneficial, and which certainly would not have happened had the All-Union Council been left to its own devices. (Compare the Orthodox Church, where the urge for reform has not yet been strong or united enough to force this issue and the crippling measures of 1961 remain unmodified.)

Secondly, the reformers syphoned off the wrath of the State

directly against themselves, thus leaving the All-Union Council with a breathing space after the tragic deterioration of the years 1959–64. Local atheists wanting to vent their spleen turned naturally to unregistered groups in the first instance. Continued protestations of loyalty by the leaders of the official Church won them the right recently to double the printing of *Fraternal Messenger*, to publish new small editions of the hymn book and Bible and, most significantly, to institute a correspondence course for the training of pastors (though there is still doubt as to whether this will become a permanent institution). The Orthodox Church won no comparable gains after 1964.

The reformers now claim (in their communiqué of May 24, 1969: "The All-Union Council does not want to admit that in the congregations under them the zeal among young people to study the Bible together and to glorify God in choral singing and instrumental music are all results of the internal Church [i.e. the reform] movement." It is possible, however, that some members of the AUCECB might make such admissions in private.

Perhaps it is in the context of the general evolution of Soviet society that the Baptist Reform Movement has had the greatest significance of all. The last decade has seen the evolution of a grass-roots human rights movement in the U.S.S.R. The process has been slow and painful, but it is now ineradicable. Already it includes hundreds of thousands of Crimean Tartars who were deported from the Crimea by Stalin and are now fighting for the right to return to it; many Ukrainians who are determined to win the right for a greater national self-determination; writers who want to be writers and not abject party hacks; scientists who disagree with the way their work is being used and want to see a complete re-thinking of Soviet (and American) foreign policy; Russian Orthodox churchmen who feel betrayed by their leaders; and ordinary citizens (like Anatoli Marchenko) who feel shamed by what happened in Czechoslovakia or who want to live and work quietly under protection from the law, not the continual threat of persecution by it.

We hear new indications from time to time that these various strands of protest are beginning to coalesce into something much bigger than any of them could ever be individually. It is surely a significant social phenomenon, and for the Christian, especially for the Baptist, a matter of some pride, that a dedicated band of religious people should have been, by example, among the founders of this movement and should have forged several new lines of action before others devised or, perhaps, even dared to think of them.

## Soviet Baptists and the West

The Christian conscience of the West is concerned about Vietnam, racial issues, world poverty and the developing nations, and Church leaders have spoken out on them forthrightly. It is both strange and sad that the whole question of human rights in the communist countries has never received any such attention. There must be some psychological explanation for this, for the facts have now been available for some years and it is no longer justifiable to fear that 'we harm the cause of Soviet Christians by taking it up', because the latter have taken the initiative out of our hands by trying to present their case to the court of world public opinion.

Vins, Kryuchkov and their followers have repeatedly appealed not only to such organizations as the Baptist World Alliance and to 'All Christians of the World'. They have also appealed to the United Nations—after all, basic issues of human rights, not just of religious freedom, were at stake. The reformers made their major drive to have their case heard at the United Nations in the summer of 1967. When no action was taken nor even any acknowledgment made of the documents drafted, Mrs. Nina Yakimenkova, a mother of seven children, risked her own freedom by going to Moscow and seeking out western correspondents. John Miller reported her as saying (*Daily Telegraph*, December 20, 1967): " 'Surely someone is listening to our appeals? Surely someone will help us? Can't you tell U Thant we have heard nothing from him?' Mrs. Yakimenkova talked unemotionally of the systematic persecution of the 'several hundred thousand' Baptists who broke with the official Baptist movement in Russia a few years ago."

Of course, Soviet membership of the United Nations has so

far paralysed the organization from giving this issue (as so many others) the airing it deserves. To turn to specifically religious organizations, the World Council of Churches, the Baptist World Alliance and other bodies are in a somewhat similar situation. Soviet citizens who represent their churches on these organizations maintain what is in effect a political veto over the agenda. Therefore in present circumstances it is impossible to have these issues publicly vented without risking that Soviet membership of them might cease.

Here it is necessary to ask disturbing questions (and by asking them, we wish to open them up for honest discussion, not to prejudge what the answers should be). For example, what have the Soviet churches gained at home in concrete terms by this membership over the last decade? Is the continuing absence of the Soviet human rights issue from the agenda justified on any terms? If a reform Baptist leader were to visit the West, would the World Council of Churches or any western Baptist movement be prepared to take advantage of his wealth of Christian experience?

Because the mainstream Churches have no policy of aid to, or even study of, the religious situation under communism, it has been left to various independent missionary organizations to act. Pressure is beginning to build up from below among ordinary church members. A number of us over the past few years have tried to help both Christian leaders and ordinary churchmen by giving them the facts while remaining as objective as is humanly possible in dealing with an emotional subject. At last there are some signs that these two approaches between them are beginning to have an effect.

For example, on November 15, 1967, the General Secretary of the British Council of Churches and one of his senior associates wrote a letter to the London *Times* pointing out the effects of Soviet atheistic policies, including a reference to the two hundred Baptists at that time in prison. The National Council of Churches (New York) followed this up very soon after by passing a resolution at its meeting in San Diego, California, on February 22, 1968, which read, in part:

In the light of these facts, the General Board of the National

Council of Churches therefore authorizes the General Secretary of the National Council of Churches to appeal to the Soviet authorities for the release of persons imprisoned in violation of religious freedom and other human rights . . .

At the same time, the General Board of the National Council of Churches desires to assure persons imprisoned or suffering for their religious faith, their families and relatives in the Soviet Union, of its prayerful concern for their ordeal and of its continuous support and lasting bond of religious fellowship and faith.

In August 1969, the head of the Anglican Communion, the Archbishop of Canterbury, wrote:

Having visited Russia twice, I feel deep fellowship with Christians in the Soviet Union who maintain their faith and hand it down to their children amidst all the pressures of atheistic propaganda. The Soviet Government professes to allow liberty of worship and is committed to it by its signature of the Human Rights Charter. Lately there have been the most painful instances of the violation of the rights of Christians to meet for worship. Let them know that we Christians in other countries are with them in our prayers, and in our protests against any violation of those rights which are professed by every state which accepts the Human Rights Charter.

On October 3, 1969, the National Council of Churches in New Zealand addressed a letter to the Religious Liberty Secretariat of the World Council of Churches, with the text of a resolution regarding the situation of 'dissenting' Baptists, Jews and other religious minorities in the Soviet Union and about religious freedom in other communist countries. The resolution stated, in part:

The National Council of Churches in New Zealand, assembled in Gisborne in July, 1969, is vitally concerned about the state of religious freedom in communist countries . . .

We are particularly anxious that dissenting Baptists in the

U.S.S.R. should have basic human rights restored to them, and that people in communist countries should become aware that the treatment of religious minorities is a matter on which Churches in other countries share a common concern ...

The tide is turning and it is no longer necessary, thank God, to deplore the total lack of concern on the part of Christians in the West as one had to do up to 1964. Let us hope that this will be expressed more and more in terms of a general concern for the establishment of human rights rather than as support by Christians for Christians. Our faith is not a club, but a commitment to human well-being.

Much as one would like to end at this point, it is not possible to do so without adding a footnote on the western Baptist reaction to the schism in the Soviet Union.

It has, not surprisingly, been a consistent part of the policy of the All-Union Council in its relations with the West to go to considerable lengths to minimize the size of this schism and conceal its true causes. Recently the present author discussed the Reform Movement with members of a Soviet Baptist group visiting the West. The delegates claimed that the author had in fact been personally informed about the schism when he last visited the Moscow Baptist Church in 1964. This was quite untrue—the author did not first hear of the schism until 1965. Yet the Soviet delegates claimed that it was the present writer who had been guilty of concealing these facts from the western public!

Contacts with foreign Christians have persistently been used to misrepresent facts, so it is perhaps not so surprising, although it is exceedingly painful, that, by and large, Baptist organizations in the West (as well as the World Council of Churches) appear to have accepted the case of the All-Union Council over against the reformers. This assumption may be unjustified, but it is the impression which has been given to a number of people. Georgi Vins has been criticized for allegedly setting out deliberately to be a martyr. Readers of this book will be able to formulate their own opinions about this.

A recent example of the way information is deliberately distorted by representatatives of the All-Union Council when travelling abroad occurred in May 1970. The *Baptist Times* wrote (May 14):

## Russian Baptists Register Churches

Russian Baptists belonging to the separated Evangelical-Baptist group (known as *Initsiativniki* Action Group) are now applying to register their churches with the state.

Mrs. Claudia Pillipuk, a member of the All-Union Council of Evangelical Christian-Baptists and of the Moscow Baptist church, gave this news to the *Baptist Times* last week.

She is on a visit to Britain with Rev. Arthur Mitskevich of Moscow and the Rev. Michael Chernopiatov, superintendent of sixty-five churches in the Tula and Vologda region, 100 miles north of Moscow (sic).

Mrs. Pillipuk said that following the triennial assembly of the Baptist Union of Russia in December, which was attended by several of the Action Group, the *Initsiativniki* held a conference of their own two days later[1] and advised their members to register their churches.

Until then they had refused to register their churches on the ground that it was a breach of the principle of complete separation of Church and State.

The *Initsiativniki* broke away from the Baptist Union on this and other issues in 1963.

Because they have attempted to worship without being registered, some hundreds of pastors and members have been fined or imprisoned during the past seven years.

"Now they are confused", said Mrs. Pillipuk.
"They say, 'If we can now register, why did we break away from the Union?'

"There is to be another meeting with leaders of the *Initsiativniki* soon and we hope that there will be a reconciliation."

1. In fact, two days before.

This report led the present author to write a letter to the Editor of the *Baptist Times*, which read as follows:

"Their leaders simply wanted to seize power for themselves". "They're a rallying-point for anti-Soviet elements among a tiny minority of our religious people." "Doctrinal extremists—they won't have fellowship with anyone who doesn't share their ultra-narrow views, not even with us."

So the slanders against the reform Baptists of the Soviet Union have been brought out in succession (sadly by other Russian Baptists) over the past decade. Thus it comes as no surprise to find that now, once again, truth is being turned on its head over the registration issue. Anyone who read the extensive documentation set out in my *Religious Ferment in Russia* (Macmillan, 1968) will find the facts set out in this matter, as in the others raised above. The truth is that the Soviet State has, right up to the present, *consistently refused* to register reform Baptist congregations, so forcing them to be illegal and then imprisoning their leaders for holding services of worship.

The basic points at issue have been: 1. the acceptance or rejection of the *Letter of Instructions* and the *New Statutes* foisted on the churches without discussion in 1960 (and later annulled); 2. the right of Baptists to elect their own representatives at all levels and govern their own affairs without State interference.

It is indeed true that the reform Baptists, as soon as their leaders could re-assemble after their long terms of imprisonment, were given official permission to confer together for the first time ever and did so on December 6, 1969, in Tula. Let us hope that the *desire* to register which they expressed (but already put forward 'continuously and insistently' by some congregations at least as early as 1961—see *Religious Ferment*, p.5) is now, at long last, going to receive a positive reaction from the authorities. If it does, this could cause a basic change for the better in the Russian Baptist situation. But it would be wise to wait for positive proof of such a major change in State policy before assuming that it is going to take place.

The editor chose not to publish the letter in full, but quoted from it. The points made in the first two paragraphs were omitted in their entirety.

Just two days after the author had written this letter, the document reached London which reported the arrest of Vins, Rumachick and Khorev and the refusal of registration to the congregation at Krivoi Rog. This immediately raised the question of the timing of the Russian visit. Was it merely a coincidence that Mrs. Pillipuk's seriously misleading words were given prominence in the Baptist press just before the breaking of the new information so detrimental to the name of the Soviet State? The visitors also gave the impression (in private conversation) that all was totally normal with Vins.

These doubts cannot be resolved, but the fact that such awkward questions have to be asked hardly fills one with confidence about the purpose of such visits.

This episode—and it is far from being an isolated one—should encourage a certain reserve in the handling of information, particularly verbal information, emanating from official Russian Baptist (and Orthodox) sources.

What, for example, is the truth about the Prokofiev affair? When he was released from prison in 1967 and sent into exile, he allegedly wrote a report retracting his former position and criticizing Kryuchkov and Vins for their continuing campaign after the Baptist Congress of 1963. Then later he retracted this report and once again threw his weight behind the reformers. We have never received the relevant documents, but there is hard evidence about the incident contained in the official *Fraternal Messenger* (No. 1, 1968, p. 70). This is part of a report by Pastor Mitskevich on the plenum of the All-Union Council which had met in Moscow in December 12–14, 1967:

> In his recent appeal to believers, A. F. Prokofiev brings up several points concerning the legislation on religious associations and continues to accuse the All-Union Council of apostasy because it observes this legislation. One can only marvel at the inconsistency of Brother Prokofiev: yesterday he renounced the mistakes of the so-called 'Council of Churches' and repented of his participation in them, yet

today he approves them. Can one follow such an inconsistent man?

We cannot expect to be able to disentangle what really happened without access to the documents themselves, but it seems quite possible that Prokofiev's intervention was caused by the machinations of someone not seeking the good of the Church. Could it have been that, in the isolation of this exile, he was visited by some emissary who furnished him with false information about the activities of Kryuchkov and Vins during Prokofiev's own imprisonment, thus leading him to renounce them? If so, this would explain his *volte-face* when he was later put in the picture.

Prokofiev has since been widely vilified for alleged immoral conduct. At one stage it was rumoured that he was living in a sinful relationship with his daughter and then, later, that he had taken a woman who was not his wife. It was for the second of these two alleged acts that the Council of Churches is reported to have excommunicated him.

It would be well to remember that Prokofiev was still serving his five years of exile in a remote area of Siberia during the whole of this time and therefore could not have free communication with anybody. It would be a wise precaution to refrain from any judgment in this matter until Prokofiev is able to speak freely for himself.

Seeing the way in which so many facts about the Reform Movement had been distorted, the present author hoped he could set the record straight by marshalling all the evidence about it which was available and printing the relevant documents virtually without commentary for his academic thesis presented to Oxford University in 1968 and published as *Religious Ferment in Russia*. Perhaps it is not without significance that, alone among reviewers, the editor of the London *Baptist Times* accused him of bias ("He continually records the position of the Action Group [reformers] in terms of virtue") and even of lack of integrity ("he omits parts of some quotations that do not suit his theme"). In his concluding sentence, the reviewer wrote: "It would be a serious matter, as well as unjust, if this book persuaded western readers to cheer one side and condemn the other." It should, however, be pointed out that since then the *Baptist Times* has frequently given news of the reformers and takes a position which is strongly critical of the restrictive Soviet laws on religion.

The prediction about cheering and condemnation did not come true (whether or not there were grounds for making it). Some people, on the contrary, still gain the impression that western Christendom has not extended its right hand of fellowship equally to all fellow-believers in the Soviet Union. Of course, every opportunity of developing official contacts must continue to be taken—but does this necessarily preclude recognition of the fact that the Council of Churches represents a large number of Baptists in the Soviet Union? Or does its outlawing by an atheist power deny such recognition? Even the prosecutor at the Vins-Kryuchkov trial was prepared to grant that the Council was representative.

Alexander Karev, moreover, at the 1966 congress, requested prayerful concern for prisoners and directed that financial sacrifices could be made according to the individual conscience.

By no means all western Christian leaders have so much as requested such prayerful concern. There have, of course, been unpublicized representations by western Church leaders, but they have not always been based upon an adequate knowledge of the facts. It may well be that agitation for a public protest has been restrained by (probably unjustified) fears of the consequences to Russian Baptists themselves—not least to the reformers. Yet, on balance, it seems that a man who is sentenced secretly in the depths of the countryside is more likely to receive a savage sentence than someone about whom there has been international publicity. The Soviet Union will always act where necessary in its own defence (witness Czechoslovakia), yet it dislikes a scandal. Would Vins have survived if there had not been publicity about his prison conditions in 1968? There can be no answer. One thing is certain: his prison conditions became no worse after the story had hit the newspapers.

Now, more and more, the whole question of whether or not to publicize is being taken out of our hands. It is the Russian Christians themselves who have already taken the decision for us. They appeal to every organization in the West which they think might possibly help their cause. Whatever the risks in doing this, they take them gladly and openly, signing documents with full names and addresses. If they do this, what right have we to deny them the publicity they seek—especially seeing the authorities would rather sentence them in decent obscurity? Or are we to censor them, claiming we know better than they what is good for them?

However, any and every action which we take must be based on a full knowledge of the facts. All prayers in our homes, all East-West Church relations furthered by our great representative bodies, should be based on this knowledge.

In conclusion, therefore, we suggest that the schism among the Russian Baptists is basically a creative one, saddening though so many of its aspects have turned out to be. The schism has demonstrated that under severe State pressure there are two possible ways to move forward: one is to make a compromise with the authorities and use the breathing space thus created with extreme caution to win quiet gains (as the All-Union Council has in fact done since 1966); the other is to take the direct approach of avoiding compromise like the plague and of using every opportunity to expose malpractices and put one's case openly to the oppressor first, then, if there is no response, to the whole world. The resolution of this dilemma is not a straight choice between right and wrong, but will be largely conditioned by temperament. There can be advantages in both.

The achievements of the All-Union Council since 1966, quiet and unspectacular though they are, are substantial ones and they give cause for joy. In 1965 nothing seemed less likely than that there would shortly be small printings of the Bible and the hymn book, an increased edition of *Fraternal Messenger*, the introduction of theological correspondence courses and the sending again of a trickle of students abroad for training.

The reformers, too, have cause for pride. They have achieved some, but not all, of the internal reforms at which they originally aimed. Perhaps more important, however, is their moral stand in face of suffering. Despite unremitting attacks in the Soviet press for their alleged 'fanaticism' (and, alas, only too frequent allegations in the West that they have gone out of their way to make trouble and court martyrdom), what is note-worthy about them most often is their restraint in the face of the most dire provocations. They have consistently eschewed 'anti-Soviet agitation', when the treatment meted out to them would have led one to expect that they would have been incited to hostility to the whole of the society around them. One combs a thousand pages of their writings in vain for passages which fall below this level of consistent Christian responsibility. Martin Luther King would have approved of them. When Vladimir Kuroyedov, the head of the government's Council for Religious Affairs, attacks them (as he has done on several oc-casions) hysteria and vehemence suppurate from his every sen-tence. The reformers' appeals to the government rarely fail to offer love to the persecutors; even where they do not, they are detailed, restrained, sober, accurate. To this day, no single fact they contain (unlike the wild rumours which circulate from other sources) has ever been disproved by the atheists in hun-dreds of newspaper attacks on them. Perhaps the appendix which follows gives the best support to date for this assertion.

There is still very, very much we do not know about the life, personality and family of Georgi Vins and Gennadi Kryuch-kov. One day perhaps the full story will be told. Meanwhile, however, we are left with a situation which they, as self-effacing Christians, would prefer. The truest record of their lives is in the Reform Movement which they led from 1962–66. Without doubt, more will be heard of them. Their utter devotion to the cause of human rights in the Soviet Union in general, and of Christian liberty in particular, undoubtedly inspires many others to follow their example. They have touched the chord of dedicated self-sacrifice in others, an utter devotion to principle and a lack of concern for personal safety. They have un-doubtedly been an inspiration to others right outside their own movement, like the recently-arrested Orthodox Christian, Boris Talantov, who referred with approval in one of his letters to the uncompromising stand of the Baptist Reform Movement.

From the crucible of their experience, Russian Christians have—and will continue to have—much to teach us all.

# APPENDIX

Extracts from an article in
*Science and Religion*, December 1969, pp. 54–57
attacking the author
Summarized passages in square brackets.

## LATTER-DAY APOSTLES OF THE BAPTIST CHURCH IN
## ANTI-SOVIET SPECULATION

by
I. Brazhnik

*Senior Lecturer of the
Philosophical Faculty of
Moscow University*

About ten years ago Michael Bourdeaux, a graduate of an Oxford theological college and a British subject, spent a year at Moscow university. Soon after his departure from Moscow, he began to publicize vigorously the situation of religion in our country, and he was later among the professional anti-communists working at the so-called 'Centre de Recherches et d'Etude des Institutions Religieuses' (Geneva, Switzerland). Bulky volumes on religion in our country issued forth from Bourdeaux's pen; *The Observer* and other newspapers have been opening their pages to him to assess this question, and he speaks on BBC programmes.

Recently Bourdeaux has been devoting particular attention to the Baptists and the book *Religious Ferment in Russia: Protestant Opposition to Soviet Religious Policy* (London 1968) is about them. He aims to give his own assessment of the state of affairs in the Evangelical Christian and Baptist Church and to present the matter as though the schism among them, the *In-*

*itsiativniki* movement (this term has been adopted to designate the followers of the so-called 'Council of Evangelical Christian and Baptist Churches'—the illegally founded and underground centre of those congregations which broke away from the All-Union Council of Evangelical Christians and Baptists)—was a consequence of changes in Soviet policy on religious matters. He claimed that the harsher State line on the Church evoked a reaction from the 'true zealots' of the Baptist-Evangelical persuasion. Thus Bourdeaux without foundation casts doubt about the assertion of Soviet authors that this movement was the result above all of a crisis, of an 'impoverishment' of faith, as recognized, incidentally, by the leaders of the *Initsiativniki* themselves.

### The 'Paradox' of Religious Consciousness and its Recognition

The author claims that the widespread secularization of religion leads to a crisis and then to its decay. This applies also to the Russian Baptists who now get most of their new members from within Baptist families.

...The 'converts' are young people who have grown up in Baptist families, who essentially *have not yet discovered their own personalities*; their parents have exploited their authority to take control of the development of their young souls.

Moreover, mass refusals on the part of these same young people to accept baptism are typical, although such a step is sometimes difficult for children and youths. Study of the composition of Baptist families (and these families have, as a rule, many children) shows that only an insignificant percentage of those children who have grown up in them follow 'the way of faith', while the majority do not accept Baptist teaching.

That is why the inference about the genuine collapse of missionary activity and the presence of a profound inner crisis in the Baptist church is justified . . .

[There arises the paradox of believers trying to reconcile the irreconcilable: religion with socialism and science—but the paradox is only apparent: this must inevitably happen and even theologians will try to rethink religious dogmas.]

Do the church leaders and theologians always recognize this 'paradox'? By no means. And even where they do, it is not in the same way; the recognition varies.

It is difficult to believe that Bourdeaux has not read *Honest to God*, a book by John Robinson, former Bishop of Woolwich, which recently appeared in England. This important, sober-minded English theologian casts doubt in his book on all the basic tenets of Christianity in order, of course, to bring it up to the contemporary level of science. He did this because he understood that: "We are on the brink of an era when it will be more and more difficult to defend the Christian faith".[1]

[Modernization and secularization occurred among Soviet Baptists in the late 'forties and the 'fifties, Brazhnik says—the conservatives refused to see this as a natural process and labelled it the result of state pressure.]

Thus the leaders of the Church have found themselves between the Scylla of modernization and the Charybdis of conservatism . . .

It is not surprising that *Initsiativniki* leaders, blinded by their own fanaticism, do not see—or rather do not want to see—the true reasons for the schism and the emergence of the new movement. But it is quite unforgivable that Bourdeaux, who aspires to the role of a researcher, does not so much as mention either the secularization and the crisis in the Baptist faith, or the search for ways out of it.

## The 'Initsiativniki': Reformers or Obscurantists? . . .

Bourdeaux states that the majority of Evangelical Christians and Baptists followed the *Initsiativniki* and on this basis he comes to the conclusion that the All-Union Council of Evangelical Christians and Baptists is an unrepresentative body. Neither can he understand why the authorities refuse to support the leaders of the *Initsiativniki*—these 'intellectuals', 'apostles of the twentieth century' and 'fighters for freedom of the spirit', as he calls them.

In fact everything is the other way round: these latter-day apostles did not find wide support among their fellow-believers. These groups of unsatisfied people who broke away from the congregation, demanding broad development of missionary activity, activization of religious education and indoctrination of children, complete isolation from 'the world', the prohibition of marriages with non-believers, etc., were not supported by the majority of believers. The *Initsiativniki* succeeded in uniting around themselves only insignificant groups of adherents.

[The 'traditionally anti-Soviet' elements in the Baptist Church seized on the new movement, Brazhnik claims—see their negative attitude to 'the world' and to all involvement in social life.]

We can add to this the enforced (and illegal!) indoctrination of children with religion—by means of instruction in circles and schools specially created for this purpose, instruction according to a programme which is in complete conflict with what is envisaged in school teaching plans.

All this is crowned by an extreme eschatological outlook, delirious expectations of the near end of the world and the Last Judgment, the demand for an almost monastic asceticism from young people, exhaustive fasts, striving for martyrdom, etc. In a word, in their obscurantism the *Initsiativniki* have surpassed the most extreme conservatives.

The highly anti-social character of their teaching is manifest in their doctrine of the sanctity of suffering, of 'the torture of the cross' as the essence and aim of human life, as a joy for the 'true Christian'. Thus they assert the inevitability of martyrdom as a consequence of serving the Church. This is precisely the reason why they aim at illegal activity, at provoking conflicts and at the exacerbation of relations with the authorities and the public—so as to deepen the gulf between the congregation and 'the world' and to strengthen the anti-social mood of believers . . .

This is confirmed by the personality of the leaders of the movement; for example, G. P. Vins's father was a presbyter and his grandfather one of the leading Baptist figures of the 'twenties, who co-operated with American missionaries and took a stand against Soviet authority.[2] The father of L. Ye. Kovalenko took an active stand against collectivization. S. T. Golev himself took part in the *kulak* rising. V. I. Kozlov was sentenced five times, for banditry, among other offences.[3] The brother and sister Unizhonny (presbyter and mistress of the Sunday school in Prokopievsk) are from a family of Bandera supporters.

But Bourdeaux 'did not notice' all this and cannot understand why atheists consider the *Initsiativniki* to be people with a negative attitude to society and to the world around them ... After all, he declares, they do not make anti-social appeals; their main theme (love your neighbour and renounce the world) comes to the fore only in that they do not allow marriages with non-believers.

### Freedom of Conscience is a Class Concept!

... The *Initsiativniki* demand that the Church be offered complete independence from the State, declaring that they can keep to State laws only if these 'do not contradict Gospel teaching'; they demand 'the liberty of organized teaching of religion to children' and also the cessation of atheist education of children in schools and of the teaching of atheism in institutes of higher education.

[The *Initsiativniki* interpret 'freedom of conscience' as 'freedom of religious profession' and 'separation of Church and State' as 'independence of the Church'.]

The real reason for Bourdeaux's interest in the *Initsiativniki* is solely this: he likes the fact that they speak out against the laws of the Soviet State and misrepresent its policy in religious matters. And Bourdeaux willingly supports them, so as to drum up mistrust in the West towards our country.

It is not by chance that the obscurantists of the American Union of Churches,[4] the anti-Soviet émigrés of *Posev* and the Ukrainian nationalists have actively supported the *Initsiativniki*. The coincidence of class interest in all these pronouncements against the Soviet State is clear.

Bourgeois operators like Bourdeaux aim to tear the religious question out of the context of the social life of the community as a whole and they regard it purely formally. The fundamentally different understanding of the term 'freedom of conscience' is evident. Bourgeois ideologists, as is well known, admit at best only religious freedom and tolerance while not allowing freedom of atheism. They call this freedom of conscience. But this is nothing other than a limitation of the concept, or rather a change of it. In reality, freedom of conscience includes the freedom of atheism. This is obligatory—it is even the chief component. Therefore freedom of conscience is realizable in all its breadth only under conditions of socialism . . .

[Capitalist states are worried by the decay of religion and the consequent emancipation of the workers, Brazhnik maintains, so they are trying to bolster up the Church. In socialist states, on the other hand, there is real freedom of atheism, and religion is necessarily prevented from encroaching on the rights of the individual.]

For us, as for our friends abroad, the words on freedom of conscience of Hewlett Johnson, the late Dean of Canterbury Cathedral, have retained their significance. He stated that communism had won a very great victory in the struggle for the liberation of the human conscience . . .

## When Religion is Used as a Weapon

It is well known that imperialist circles of the West in their ideological subversions against our country attribute a large role to religion also—to its revival and activization among Soviet people and to its exploitation for anti-socialist ends.

Through the solicitude of various imperialist funds, 'institutes' and 'centres' have been formed which concern themselves with gathering information and falsifying materials, using them for anti-Soviet purposes. Their chief task is, first, to misrepresent religious policy in the U.S.S.R. to public opinion in the West and, second, to attempt to create with the help of religion a social stratum hostile to the Soviet order. The links between the intelligence services of bourgeois countries and such centres have been revealed in print. For example, the English General Dixon and Dr. Helbrunn have defined as the first principle for agents of imperialist states finding collaborators in communist countries among religious people.

It is to this aspect of the question that we would like to draw the attention of those of the *Initsiativniki* who still listen to the voice of their leaders. One of them (G. Vins), by the way, refused to believe that one of the letters signed by him and G. Kryuchkov had been reprinted by *Posev*—the organ of the NTS[5]—one of the most hostile anti-Soviet émigré publications.

*Posev* has printed several slanderous letters by the *Initsiativniki* with appropriate commentaries and far-reaching conclusions. The same also happened with other anti-Soviet publications, a number of which, as well is known, are financed by the Central Intelligence Agency of the U.S.A. As for the rabidly anti-Soviet journal of the Ukrainian Baptist-nationalists, *Messenger of Truth* (*!?*) published in the U.S.A., it called I. Bondarenko 'the Billy Graham of the Ukraine'—the same Graham who is distinguished by his anti-communism, his support of racism and American aggression in Vietnam ... We might add that this journal recently buried alive G. Vins and I. Bondarenko, who were perfectly healthy and at liberty, reporting on their death 'in prison from starvation'!

The English writer, James Aldridge, is profoundly right to warn those who do not see the way the reactionaries are exploiting these latest methods of using 'God as a weapon and the power of journalism as a hangman's noose' in order to achieve their aims.

Recently in the anti-Soviet press it has become fashionable to speak from the would-be 'objective' position of being apparently favourably disposed towards the Soviet people, utilising everything that might lend an appearance of reliability and of a documentary basis to an anti-Soviet concoction. This is the category to which Bourdeaux's work belongs. He uses an arsenal of methods to force the reader to believe him.

Of course the reader who is poorly informed on the question under consideration may be impressed by the author's factual knowledge, by the abundance of documents that he quotes, by a mass of footnotes. Such a demonstration of the author's erudition is calculated to impress the ignorant man and convince him of the justice of Bourdeaux's anti-Soviet ideas. It is, to be frank, not a new method.

His second method is not original, either: the cowardly

avoidance of polemics with Soviet specialists—for the simple reason that no objection can be made to their essential position. 'None so deaf as he who will not hear', aptly says the English proverb.

There is no doubt that Bourdeaux's writings do not bring honour to the Church which has nurtured him, nor to the college within whose walls he was educated. But we are not personally concerned with the question of whether they bear legal or moral responsibility for such activities of his.

It is, however, a matter for concern to Soviet people that Bourdeaux is trying to present the policy of the Soviet State in religious matters in a false light to western readers.

We have not set ourselves in this article to convince Mr. Bourdeaux of his error; that would, doubtless, be a fruitless task. We were concerned to show why such books appear, how they are put together, by what methods the poverty of the argument and the bourgeois class position of the authors is concealed, the more so since Bourdeaux's scribbles reflect a definite direction in the arsenal of imperialist propaganda, poisoning the minds of people in the West with the venom of anti-Soviet ideas.

## NOTES

1. This is a re-translation from the Russian. The original in English reads: "For I suspect that we stand on the brink of a period in which it is going to become increasingly difficult to know what the true defence of Christian truth requires" (translator's note).

2. Brazhnik's own knowledge of the facts here appears to be hazy.

3. Kozlov has now told the remarkable story of his conversion to Christianity and a new life while in prison on criminal charges. Text available from the Centre for the Study of Religion and Communism.

4. No such body is known to exist. Both the anti-communist International Council of Christian Churches and the far more representative National Council of Churches have passed resolutions criticizing Soviet persecution of Baptists.

5. National Labour Union.

# FOR FURTHER READING ON
# RELIGION IN THE USSR

*General*

RELIGION IN THE USSR, ed. Boris Iwanow, Munich, 1960.

RELIGION IN THE SOVIET UNION, by Walter Kolarz, London, 1961.

OPIUM OF THE PEOPLE, by Michael Bourdeaux, London, 1965.

RELIGION AND THE SEARCH FOR NEW IDEALS IN THE USSR, ed. W. Fletcher & A. Strover, New York and London, 1967.

RELIGION IN THE USSR, ed. Robert Conquest, London, 1968.

RUSSIANS OBSERVED, by Sir John Lawrence, London, 1969.

RELIGION AND THE SOVIET STATE: A DILEMMA OF POWER, ed. M. Hayward & W. Fletcher, London, 1969.

RELIGIOUS MINORITIES IN THE SOVIET UNION (1960–70), ed. Michael Bourdeaux, London, 1970.

*Protestants*

THE CHRISTIANS FROM SIBERIA, by J. C. Pollock, London, 1964.

RELIGIOUS FERMENT IN RUSSIA, by Micheal Bourdeaux, London, 1968.

CHRISTIAN APPEALS FROM RUSSIA, ed. R. Harris & Xenia Howard-Johnston, London, 1969.

RUSSIAN CHRISTIANS ON TRIAL, ed. and translated by Michael Bourdeaux and Kathleen Matchett, London, 1970.

*Russian Orthodox Church*

CHRISTIANS IN CONTEMPORARY RUSSIA, by Nikita Struve, London, 1967.

NIKOLAI, by W. C. Fletcher, London, 1968.

THE RECENT ACTIVITIES OF THE MOSCOW PATRIARCHATE ABROAD AND IN THE USSR, by John Dunlop, Seattle, 1970.

PATRIARCH AND PROPHETS: PERSECUTION OF THE RUSSIAN ORTHO-DOX CHURCH TODAY, by Michael Bourdeaux, London, 1970.

*Jews*

THE JEW IN SOVIET RUSSIA SINCE 1971, ed. Lionel Kochan, London, 1970.

All the above are available through the Centre for the Study of Religion and Communism.

# AUTHOR'S POSTSCRIPT

If you feel moved by this book, if you feel that Russian Christians are important and you want to know more about them, then the work of the Centre for the Study of Religion and Communism will be of interest to you.

No university or religious organization has ever undertaken a full enquiry into the situation of the Churches in communist countries—strange when you think of the amount of public attention which has been paid to so many other aspects of human rights. Yet over the last few years more and more people have been coming to realize that there is a deficiency here. The Centre, therefore, is coming into existence as a direct response to a need which has been widely expressed.

We believe that we can help by making the situation of Christians living under communism better known. We believe that such publicity must be objective, factual and extending to other religions than Christianity. We are exploring every possible means of increasing this publicity, both in more popular ways, such as journalism, radio and TV, and through the less ephemeral medium of printed books.

Much research in recent years has led to an awareness of the need for and to the formation of the Centre. In the first few weeks of its life it has produced on commission *Religious Minorities in the Soviet Union* (1960–1970) and *Russian Christians on Trial*, both listed above. The Centre's honorary Director, the author of this book, receives a research grant from the Centre for International Studies at the London School of Economics and Political Science, which ensures that our work is being used by the universities. For example, Glasgow University regularly publishes our summaries of articles on religion from the Soviet press. We are already putting out all the best of our information to those who subscribe to our mailing list or who financially support the work of the Centre.

Up to a few years ago the 'Church of Silence' was a name frequently given to Christians living under communism. They are silent no longer. They have found their voice, which may be distinctly, though distantly, heard. The Centre believes that these people have a right to speak for themselves, even though in their own countries they cannot publish what they write. One of the Centre's aims is to act as a sounding-board for them—to sponsor publication of what they are saying in the way they themselves want to say it. Readers will have noticed how much space has been given to these uncensored voices in this book. The publication of the long extracts from Ilya Brazhnik's article (Appendix) without comment demonstrates that we wish to hear what communists have to say, too. There is a debate going on here which is of immense importance to the Christian world as a whole—and the Centre for the Study of Religion and Communism is the only organization in the world geared to informing a wide public of the issues at stake.

The Centre is completely independent. Its policy is controlled solely by its Council of Management: Sir John Lawrence, O.B.E., BART. (Chairman), Professors Geoffrey Goodwin and Leonard Schapiro, the Very Rev. Kallistos Ware, Canon David Paton, the Revs. John Arnold, Alan Booth, Michael Bourdeaux, Messrs. Alexander Lieven, Peter Reddaway, Janis Sapiets and Charles Spencer.

The publication of factual information can—and does—have a directly beneficial effect in favour of those organizations which put the accent on direct relief work: it also ensures a better climate of opinion for the future. The Centre is aware of this important side effect of its work as it prepares plans for launching its Public Appeal, the main aims of which will be:

(1) To establish the work at present being done in a permanent building, which will house all the Centre's documentation and will be accessible to interested visitors.

(2) To secure permanence for the work already being done by the Centre's nucleus staff of three.

(3) To step up the Centre's publishing, especially with a regular journal, so that it is not entirely dependent on commissions from commercial publishers and other organizations.

(4) As soon as possible to increase the scope of the Centre's work and employ more research staff who will study other communist countries. (It has necessarily had to concentrate mainly upon the Soviet Union up to now, though some interesting information on other countries has been incidentally collected.)

If you would like to know more about the Centre's work and to be in regular touch with it, please write to:

> THE REV. MICHAEL BOURDEAUX,
> CENTRE FOR THE STUDY OF RELIGION AND COMMUNISM,
> 34 LUBBOCK ROAD,
> CHISLEHURST, KENT.

4 February 1971